THE
MICROWAVE
PLANNER

By the same author:

Microwave Cooking Properly Explained
Microwave Recipes For One

In the same series

Front Cover
Recipe: Beef Stew with Herb Dumplings (page 85)
Photographer: Michael Kay, Solar Studios, Croydon
Microwave Cooker: Panasonic
Home Economist: Annette Yates

THE
MICROWAVE
PLANNER

How To Adapt Your Family Favourites

Annette Yates

RIGHT WAY

Copyright notice

© Elliot Right Way Books MCMLXXXVI
First published in the *Right Way* series © MCMXCVI

Typeset in 11/12pt Times by County Typesetters, Margate, Kent.

Printed and bound in Great Britain by Cox & Wyman Ltd., Reading, Berkshire.

The *Right Way* series is published by Elliot Right Way Books, Brighton Road, Lower Kingswood, Tadworth, Surrey, KT20 6TD, U.K. For information about our company and the other books we publish, visit our web site at www.right-way.co.uk

CONTENTS

ACKNOWLEDGEMENTS

I would like to record my sincere thanks to the following people and companies.

For the use of microwave cookers: Panasonic UK Ltd, Willoughby Road, Bracknell, Berkshire, RG12 8FP; Samsung Electronics UK Ltd, 225 Hook Rise South, Surbiton, Surrey, KT6 7LD; Sharp Electronics, Sharp House, Thorp Road, Manchester, M10 9BE.

For the use of microwave cookware supplied by the mail order specialists: Lakeland Plastics Ltd, Alexandra Buildings, Windermere, Cumbria, LA23 1BQ.

For the use of an extensive range of microwave cooking utensils: Newell UK Ltd, Unit 21, Eyncourt Road, Woodside Estate, Dunstable, Bedfordshire, LU5 4TS.

For their advice: The Microwave Association, 26 Cranbourne Crescent, Parkstone, Poole, Dorset, BH13 4EP.

For patiently deciphering and typing my scribbled pages: Angela Sheldrake.

This book is dedicated to my parents, John and Olive, who are 'always here' in Cefn Coed, near Merthyr Tydfil.

INTRODUCTION

If you are a microwave owner who still has to *plan* to use the microwave cooker, then this book has been specially written for you. It 'ties up the loose ends' of microwave cooking, helping you to adapt your own everyday dishes – those family favourites that you prepare without thinking with the hob, grill or conventional oven – for cooking in the microwave. In this book I am not concerned with the microwave and how it works, or with cooking charts for basic foods. All this and more has been covered in my other books, *Microwave Cooking Properly Explained* and *Microwave Recipes for One*.

This book is the result of considerable research and is based on questions and suggestions put to me by many, many microwave owners (and prospective owners) in various parts of the country. It is based also on surveys of everyday meals prepared by family members, friends, colleagues and participants in my cookery classes – meals prepared regularly every week or at least once a month, as well as those prepared every now and again as a family treat. Hints and tips fill the pages from cover to cover, from alphabetical lists for everyday cooking, to meal plans and work plans which should help to boost your confidence in using your microwave, while utilising your time to the best advantage.

When we first learn to cook conventionally, whether it is at school, at home with parents, or when we set up our first home, all the basics have to be learned and many skills acquired. When we make mistakes we cannot always give up (after all, we all have to eat!). We keep trying other methods, other foods, and other recipes, at least until we gain an acceptable repertoire.

On the way to whatever standard of cooking we may

individually achieve, certain things become automatic – for example, *knowing* whether to use a saucepan or a frying pan, or the grill. The aim of this book is to show you when, *automatically*, it is to the microwave that you can turn. My aim is to help you reach the point where the microwave fits naturally into your system of cooking and complements (rather than competes with) the other cooking equipment in your kitchen – whether you are cooking for one or two, a family, or for large numbers of people.

The Microwave Planner is for readers who think of their microwave cookers in terms of 'I should use it more often . . . but have not got things quite together yet . . . because I never get the time to . . . understand it all . . .' I do hope this book will become their helping hand.

Whether you are a new owner of a microwave or a more experienced user, Chapter 5, Using The Recipes, is essential reading.

Bon appétit.

Annette Yates

1

MICROWAVE COOKWARE

The dishes used in microwave cookers must allow microwaves to pass through them into the food. Metal is not suitable – it reflects microwaves, so the food inside does not heat up. Microwave energy reflecting off a metal container could cause sparks which damage the microwave, so (unless your instruction book recommends it) metal and foil containers should not be used. Dishes or plates with silver or gold decorations will also cause sparking – and the metal trim will blacken. However, an exception to not using metal in the microwave cooker is the occasional use of foil to shield small areas of food (such as the wing tips on a chicken, for example) from over-cooking. Always follow your manufacturer's instructions carefully regarding the use of foil and never let it touch the walls of the microwave.

So what can we use in the microwave? We can use most ordinary household materials: *ovenglass*, *glass ceramic*, *glazed pottery* and *stoneware*. Dishes used for cooking must be able to withstand the heat created by the food inside it. For this reason paper, plastic, baskets and wood should only be used for heating for very short periods. Kitchen paper can be used to absorb moisture during microwaving but don't use the recycled variety as it may contain minute traces of metal.

There is a great variety of *microwave cookware* which is specially designed for microwave cooking – in heat-resistant plastic, glass and ceramic. When buying new cooking equipment, check that it is suitable for the microwave. If your model has a turntable, make sure the cookware fits on it, and that it will turn freely. Thankfully, much of today's cookware is suitable for the freezer, the conventional oven (up to a specific temperature), the microwave and the dishwasher. Check whether dishes are suitable for cooking foods with a high fat or sugar content and which will reach a high temperature, for example for Christmas pudding – not all plastic containers are suitable. Look out for useful starter sets of microwave cookware – an economical way of buying the most useful items.

Microwave bags and roasting bags make ideal cooking containers and can be used in the freezer too. They are light and easy to handle. Remember to tie them loosely (with string, not metal ties), or loosely tuck the open ends under the food, to allow steam to escape. Ordinary plastic food bags are not suitable for microwave cooking.

Cling film can be used to cover dishes, but do not allow it to touch the food. Pierce it to allow steam to escape. Do not be tempted to line dishes with cling film.

To test if a container is suitable for microwave use
Maybe you have some dishes in the cupboard and you are unsure whether they are suitable for microwave cooking. Try this test. Place the dish in the microwave and sit a cup or suitable container of cold water with about 150ml/¼ pt inside it. Microwave on HIGH/100% for 1–2 minutes. The outer dish should remain cool while the water in the cup has become hot. If the outer dish warms up, it is not a good idea to use it in the microwave.

Cut down on the washing-up by cooking and serving (and perhaps freezing) in the same container or by mixing and cooking in the same dish. Flameproof dishes can be used for browning (meat, for example) on the hob or under the grill and then put into the microwave to finish cooking.

Note
Do not use containers which have been repaired with glue – the glue may melt. Also, a mixing bowl with rubber on its base should not be put in a microwave – the rubber may melt.

The shape of the container is important
Round containers are best because the microwaves can penetrate equally to all sides of the food. The centre usually cooks more slowly than the outer edges, but stirring food during cooking helps to prevent this and to encourage even cooking.

A *ring shape* is very useful for foods which cannot be stirred during cooking, e.g. cakes. The slow-cooking centre has been removed.

Squares and rectangles receive extra microwave energy at their corners, causing over-cooking in foods which cannot be stirred. A rectangular dish also has a slow-cooking centre.

A *bowl* is a useful container – it has no corners so the microwaves enter the food fairly evenly. It is particularly suitable for foods which cannot be stirred (sponge puddings, for instance) and for sauces.

Containers with *sloping sides* (where the top is wider than the bottom) have extra microwave energy entering the food near the top edges and this area cooks first. It is difficult to achieve even cooking in this type of container, so choose one with vertical sides.

Microwave accessories
Over the years I have tried many microwave accessories. Here are some of the more useful ones.

Rack or trivet
These are very useful for microwaving all types of food. Use them to lift dishes off the floor of the cooker (I use them on a turntable too) so that microwaves can easily reach underneath the food as well as the top and sides. This way the food thaws or cooks more evenly. In microwave cookers with metal turntables, it is particularly important to raise the food and these cookers usually have a special rack supplied with them. Simply sit the food or dish on the rack. They are also useful for cooking joints of

meat – the meat is raised above its juices, to promote 'roasting' rather than 'stewing'.

Large jug
A large jug is an asset when making sauces, which must have space to boil up during cooking. Even a small amount of sauce boils up alarmingly, particularly if it contains milk. A good size jug also allows plenty of room for stirring or whisking sauces before, during and after cooking.

Plate ring
This is useful for stacking plated meals for thawing or reheating. One plate ring is sufficient – best (most even) results are obtained if no more than two plates are thawed and/or reheated at one time.

Microwave thermometer
This is particularly helpful for successful thawing and cooking of meat and poultry and is specially designed for use while the microwaves are switched on. Other thermometers should *only* be used while the microwave cooker is switched off. Some microwave cookers have a special thermometer or probe attached to the cooker cavity. It is inserted into the food during cooking and the microwaves switch off automatically when it has reached the required temperature.

Browning dish
This has a special coating which heats up in the microwave (see page 24 for details).

2
THAWING FOOD

The ability to thaw foods in minutes is one of the great advantages of the microwave. The need for advance meal planning is not so urgent, and it matters little if you forget to take food out of the freezer or if unexpected guests turn up on your doorstep. A meal can still be ready for eating in next to no time.

The DEFROST or MEDIUM-LOW setting is used to thaw frozen foods. This usually applies microwave energy to the food in short bursts – a clever technique since a continuous burst of microwaves would result in areas of melted food heating up while adjacent parts are still frozen. The DEFROST/MEDIUM-LOW control ensures even thawing, allowing heat from the melting parts to be conducted to the colder areas during the rest periods when the microwave energy is off. The chart on page 29 shows the percentage of the cooker power used on this setting.

Generally, thawed foods require a *defrosting-standing time* when the temperature inside the food is allowed to even out and any remaining ice crystals can melt normally. By allowing for this defrosting-standing time you will make sure that thawing is even and that the food does not begin to heat up or cook at its edges. Many microwave cookers have an AUTO-DEFROST setting which is controlled by time, during which the microwaves start thawing on a high power, gradually reducing to the lowest power, to thaw the food efficiently. It is designed so that the thawing times effectively include a *defrosting-standing time*.

Some models have AUTO-DEFROST which is weight-controlled – taking the guesswork out of thawing. You program in the type and weight of food and the cooker automatically calculates the thawing time (and often the defrost-standing time). In the latest models you simply put the food in the microwave and a crystal beneath the turntable automatically calculates the weight of the food and its thawing time.

Not all foods need thawing however. Some can be cooked from frozen. Vegetables are the best example. To ensure even thawing and cooking, stir or shake them once or twice during microwaving.

Thawing tips

Microwave-to-freezer containers save washing-up. Cook, freeze, thaw and reheat in the same container.

Freeze food in shallow blocks – they will thaw more quickly.

Remove metal ties, foil or foil containers before thawing.

Open containers and bags before thawing to prevent them splitting or bursting open. The air inside will expand as it warms up.

Remove any lumps of ice attached to the food – they will only slow down (and water down the food during) the thawing process.

Remove giblets from inside poultry as soon as possible.

Place cakes, bread and pastries on kitchen paper during thawing, so excess moisture is soaked up.

Thaw frozen foods in a close-fitting dish. If the thawed areas are allowed to spread over the base of a container they will attract more of the microwave energy and consequently over-heat. It is a good idea to line the container with a roasting bag, or microwave bag, before adding food which is to be frozen. This way the frozen

block can be lifted out and packed away in the freezer –
useful if you don't have a never-ending supply of
microwave-freezer dishes.

Cover foods (except baked foods such as cakes, bread and
pastries) to hold in the heat and speed up the thawing
time.

Follow manufacturer's instructions for thawing times until
you are familiar with your microwave. It is a good idea to
note down times for quantities of food which you will
regularly wish to thaw.

Separate large pieces of food such as sausages and chops
as they thaw, to encourage quick, even thawing. Break up
blocks of food (such as sauces and soups) as they soften.

Turn over large or dense pieces of food (such as meat
joints, chops, poultry) half way through thawing.

Make sure poultry and meat are *completely* thawed before
cooking.

Use a microwave thermometer to tell you when the centre
of a joint has thawed.

3

REHEATING FOOD

Microwave cookers are ideal for reheating cooked food fast. The colour, flavour and texture are often just like the freshly-cooked version. Individual portions are heated up speedily – a plated meal takes just 3–4 minutes on HIGH (100%). A family-sized casserole takes about 10 minutes on HIGH (100%).

When reheating food in the microwave, rules similar to those for cooking apply.

★ The *starting temperature* of the food will dictate its reheating time, e.g. food from the refrigerator will take longer than food at room temperature.

★ *Cover* or wrap foods during reheating to retain heat and moisture. Do not cover bread, pastry or crumble toppings.

★ *Stir* sauces, soups, casseroles, milk puddings etc. to ensure even heating. *Turn or rearrange* larger items such as chicken pieces, whole potatoes or corn-on-the-cob, lasagne and shepherd's pie.

★ *Arrange* foods with care. (See page 21.) Foods on a plate should be arranged in one even layer, with thicker, denser items around the outer edge. For example, meat slices reheat very quickly and these are best placed in the centre of the plate. Reheat two meals at a time by using a plate ring – they will take 5–7 minutes depending on the food. Rotate the plates (in opposing directions) once during reheating.

★ *Avoid* reheating large, solid foods – a large piece of

meat, for instance, reheats more successfully if it is cut into slices.

★ *Under-estimate* reheating times if you are unsure. The food can easily be put back into the microwave for a little longer and still takes only minutes, but over-cooked food can dry up and spoil.

★ Make sure that reheated food is *piping hot* throughout.

★ *Use a thermometer* to check that large items are sufficiently heated to a temperature which is safe to eat. Either use a microwave thermometer (see page 80) during reheating or check the temperature regularly with a meat thermometer (but do not leave it in the microwave while it is switched on.)

★ Some foods *improve* with reheating. Slightly stale bread freshens up on reheating. Casseroles and soups often improve their flavour on reheating – they have had time for all the flavours to develop and inter-mingle.

★ *Take care* when reheating pastry with a filling. While the pastry may feel warm, the inside will be much hotter. To avoid burning the mouth, allow a standing time for the temperature in the pie to even out before serving.

★ Some foods benefit from reheating on a MEDIUM-LOW (30%) or MEDIUM (50%) setting. Vegetables (without accompanying meat or sauce) and slices of sponge or Christmas pudding are good examples. Large pieces of food which cannot be stirred (like lasagne) should be reheated on MEDIUM (50%). Foods with plenty of moisture and foods which can be stirred are usually suitable for reheating on HIGH (100%).

★ Always allow food to *stand* after reheating – to allow the temperature in the food to even out.

4

ADAPTING YOUR OWN RECIPES FOR MICROWAVE COOKING

Many of your own everyday recipes will be suitable for cooking in the microwave. Here are some general guidelines.

Timing
The obvious difference between microwave cooking and conventional cooking is the timing. As a general rule, cook your favourite recipes for one quarter to one third of their usual cooking time. For example, a dish which takes 40 minutes to cook conventionally may take about 12 minutes to cook in the microwave. There will, of course, be foods which do not fit into this rule so it is a good idea to under-estimate times and check the dish often when trying it for the first time. Remember that under-cooked food can be put back in the microwave to finish cooking, but over-cooked food cannot be corrected. Compare the cooking time of your recipe with a similar one in your manufacturer's instruction book. After all, no one knows your particular model better than its manufacturer. Always be guided by this until you are confident of success. Use the ingredient with the longest cooking time as your guide to overall timing too.

It is worth remembering that the following points will affect the timing:

★ *The type of food.* Foods containing moisture generally cook better than dry ones. The more moisture the food contains the longer it will take. Adding water to moist foods also lengthens the cooking time. Dense foods take longer than porous foods – for instance, a solid piece of meat takes longer than the same quantity of minced meat. Extra cooking time on a low power will be needed for tenderising tougher cuts of meat or for foods which need to absorb a lot of moisture (for example, rice and dried foods). Foods which usually require gentle, slow cooking when prepared conventionally should be cooked on MEDIUM (50%).

★ *The quantity of food.* Two whole potatoes will take longer than one (though not twice the time) because the microwave energy has to be shared between the two items. If your microwave has a shelf, two layers of food can be cooked, but again the cooking time will be longer. On the whole, food on the lower level tends to cook more slowly, so foods with shorter cooking times should be positioned there. Generally though, avoid filling the microwave with food – with whole potatoes for example. It is usually quicker to heat or cook them in small amounts.

★ *Its shape and thickness.* Perhaps the most important point to remember when preparing ingredients is to cut all meat and vegetables into even sizes, as regular shapes cook more evenly. It is a good idea therefore to bone and roll irregular-shaped joints of meat. Thinner pieces of food cook faster than thick ones so, when appropriate, cut large pieces into smaller pieces to allow the microwaves to penetrate them faster.

★ *The arrangement of the food.* If meat slices or pieces of fish are piled up in a cooking container they will cook unevenly. Make sure they are evenly distributed in the container. Arrange wedge-shaped foods with the tail end towards the centre (e.g. asparagus, small fish fillets). Tuck the thin ends of fish fillets under each other and overlap fish tails to produce a more even layer of food. When putting cooked meals on a plate for reheating later, make sure the arrangement is even (with no high piles of potatoes, for example, and with delicate foods, such as meat slices, placed in the centre of the plate).

★ *Its starting temperature.* Food at room temperature will cook in less time than food from the refrigerator or freezer. Cooking times given in this book are for foods at room temperature. Check that the food is cooked after the minimum time – it can always be microwaved for a little longer if necessary. Do, however, make sure that the food is piping hot throughout.

★ *The container used* and its shape in particular. A regular shape with vertical sides is best (see Chapter 1).

★ *The power level used.* Power levels enable you to adjust the amount of microwaves entering the food. Use the chart on page 29 as a guide.

Some microwave cookers incorporate sensors. These devices enable the cooker to switch off when the food is cooked – by sensing its temperature, either on its surface, or in the surrounding atmosphere. Other cookers may include computerised programs for specified weights of individual foods or made-up dishes. Check to see if the food or dish you are preparing is included in these. If not, then use the manual settings, following the advice given above.

Cooking-Standing Time
Always allow for a cooking-standing time. Food continues to cook after the microwaves are switched off as the heat is conducted from the hot outer areas of the food to the cooler central areas. Large dense foods require longer cooking-standing times. Joints of meat, for instance, will keep hot and go on conducting heat to the centre for 15 to 30 minutes after the microwave energy is switched off.

Other foods may need only a few minutes cooking-standing time, e.g. scrambled egg could be removed from the microwave when it is still slightly wet and under-cooked – by the time it is served, it will have finished cooking and firmed up.

With a little patience and practice, cooking times will become second nature and you will begin to gauge small differences automatically.

Turning and Stirring Food

Food cooked in a microwave needs to be turned and/or stirred to ensure even cooking. Avoid positioning small pieces of food in a circle with one in the centre – the one in the centre will tend not to cook. Soups, vegetables, sauces and casseroles need to be stirred occasionally to encourage even cooking. Turn foods like whole fish, chicken pieces and whole potatoes once during cooking and re-position foods such as meatballs from the outside of the dish to the centre.

Drinks should always be stirred before putting them in the microwave and part way through heating, to prevent them suddenly bubbling over.

Browning Food

Generally speaking, food cooked by microwaves does not brown. Unlike conventional cooking, the heat which cooks the food is not directed on to its surface, so it does not dry out, harden and brown. This 'drawback' seems to become less important as you get to know your micro-wave, improve your methods, use attractive garnishes and even change your attitude to crisp and browned food. You will probably find that you prefer some foods without browned surfaces. Fish, vegetables, soups, sauces, casser-oles and puddings are all good examples of foods which do not need browning but which cook superbly in the microwave.

Many microwave cookers have a browning element, or grill, which can be used to brown the tops of dishes. A combination cooker cooks with microwaves and convected heat simultaneously – producing crisp, brown foods in a fraction of the conventional cooking time.

Browning dishes

These are designed specifically for microwaves. They are the only containers which can be heated empty in the microwave. Their special coating absorbs the microwaves (on HIGH/100%), reaching a temperature of up to 300°C/600°F. The food (particularly meat, sausages, eggs, fish, vegetables and toasted sandwiches) is placed on the hot surface to sear and brown. Cooking is then completed by microwaving in the same dish. Always use oven gloves when using a browning dish, and protect your work surfaces with a heat-resistant layer before placing the hot dish on them.

Follow manufacturer's instructions carefully when using browning dishes and never exceed the recommended pre-heating time.

Microwave and Roasting bags

These are excellent for cooking larger joints of meat and whole poultry in the microwave. Tie the bag loosely to allow steam to escape during cooking. To promote browning, allow plenty of air between the meat and the bag and allow space for the bag to expand during cooking. It is a good idea to slit the bag in several places under the joint and then place the meat on a rack in a tray – as the meat cooks, the juices drain away. Alternatively, split the bag open and use it to cover the joint (which is placed on a rack), tucking the ends under.

Using roasting bags in combination cookers can help to keep the cooker walls clean and free from splashes. Follow the advice in your microwave instruction book (see page 20).

Browning agents

These can be used to produce an appearance similar to conventionally cooked food. My feeling is that we should not be imitating conventional cooking but rather exploring and appreciating the microwave's potential. However, browning agents are available for sprinkling or spreading on to food. Some of these flavour the food too, so they should be chosen with care to complement the food.

Sauces such as soy, barbecue, brown, fruity, and Worcestershire can be used, as can soup and gravy mixes or stock cubes or granules. However each of these will alter the natural flavours and should be used carefully. Paprika mixed with melted butter gives excellent results when brushed over whole chicken. Glazes using honey, jams, chutneys, mustard, soy sauce or tomato purée look (and taste) good on pieces of chicken, beef, lamb or pork.

Toppings and colourings
Dishes such as casseroles and sauce-covered vegetables can be made more attractive in various ways. They can be browned under the grill before serving (make sure the container is suitable). Alternatively, sprinkle them with toasted or fried breadcrumbs, grated cheese (particularly Parmesan), chopped fresh herbs, chopped nuts or grilled or fried bacon pieces.

Sweet dishes can be topped with brown sugar, chopped nuts, ground spices and so on. The colour of cakes can be improved by using wholewheat flour, treacle, brown sugar, spices, chocolate, cocoa or coffee in the ingredients. Simple decorations such as a sprinkling of icing sugar or cocoa powder will disguise a pale surface, as will the addition of icing with chopped nuts, grated chocolate, glacé cherries, etc.

Healthy Eating with your Microwave
Current nutritional advice emphasises the need to eat plenty of starchy foods (bread, rice, pasta, potatoes) and fresh fruit and vegetables, with moderate amounts of meat, fish, poultry, eggs and dairy foods. At the same time, we should be easing up on our intake of fat (saturated fats in particular), sugar and salt.

Whether you are on a strict diet – such as low-calorie, low-fat, salt-free – or whether you are generally aiming for a healthy diet, the microwave can be an asset.

Foods cooked in the microwave often retain more of their flavour than foods cooked conventionally. Not only do they cook quickly so there is less chance of destroying vitamins, but also the majority of foods can be cooked using little (and sometimes no) liquid, with less chance of washing away certain vitamins.

Since foods mainly cook in their own juiccs there is hardly ever need to add fat in microwave cooking. The true fresh flavours are retained and foods do not stick to the cooking containers.

Individual portions are quick and easy in the microwave, involving less effort (and fewer cooking utensils) than conventional cooking. So if someone in your family is trying to cut down on calories, fat, or sugar, for example, it need not entail the preparation of a special menu for one. In fact, as time goes by, you will probably discover that you have slowly moved over to a more healthy diet as you increase the number of dishes prepared in your microwave.

Checklist for Converting Recipes for Microwave Cooking
Finally, here is a checklist for cooking your favourite recipes in the microwave. Where it is appropriate, I have included the page number for more detailed information on this advice. You will also find handy checklists at the beginning of each section throughout the book.

For more details

★ Reduce the cooking time to about one third.   Page 20

★ Cook for the minimum time, rather than over-cook – check the cooking progress often until you are confident and ensure that the food is piping hot throughout.   Page 20

★ Check with a similar recipe in your
instruction book.   Page 20

★ Cut ingredients into even sizes.   Page 21

★ Reduce the liquid in soups and casseroles by
about a quarter. If necessary add extra   Page 46
during or after cooking.   Page 78

★ Use little or no fat. It is not needed to
brown or to prevent sticking.   Page 26

★ Use less salt and spicy seasonings. Adjust
seasoning after cooking if necessary.

★ Choose your power level.   Page 29

★ Arrange food evenly.   Page 21

★ Stir or cover foods which would normally
need stirring or covering during   Page 30
conventional cooking.   Page 23

★ Add delicate or quick-cooking ingredients
towards the end of cooking.

★ Use quick-cooking or ready-cooked
alternatives when possible, e.g. canned
kidney beans and quick-cooking rice.

★ When doubling recipe quantities, increase
the cooking time by a quarter to one third.

★ When halving recipe quantities, decrease the
cooking time by about one third.

5
USING THE RECIPES –
VITAL TO ALL READERS

Cooking Times
Cooking times given in this book apply to a 600–700W microwave cooker. If your model differs in output, adjust the timings accordingly. Here is a brief guide:

up to 600W	600–700W	750W and over
40 sec.	30 sec.	20 sec.
1½ min.	1 min.	50 sec.
4 min.	3 min.	2½ min.
6½ min.	5 min.	4 min.
13½ min.	10 min.	8½ min.
20 min.	15 min.	12½ min.
27 min.	20 min.	16½ min.

In the recipes most cooking is on HIGH (100%) unless otherwise stated.

Variable Powers
Alternatively, if your microwave has a higher wattage (750W or more) simply use a lower power level which is the equivalent of 600–700W (check with your instruction book) and cook for the recommended time.

Opposite is a general guide to power settings and their uses.

Measures
Measurements are given in metric and imperial. Use one type for best results.

Spoon measurements are level unless otherwise stated.

Eggs used are size 3 unless otherwise stated.

Power Level:	LOW 10%	MEDIUM-LOW 30%	MEDIUM 50%	MEDIUM-HIGH 70-75%	HIGH 100%
Equivalent watts (approximate):	60–70W	200–250W	300–350W	400–525W	600–700W
Use for:	Keeping food warm. Softening butter. Melting chocolate. Rising yeast doughs. Very gentle thawing.	Thawing. Gentle simmering. Developing the flavour of sauces and casseroles. Gentle cooking of casseroles, soups, custards, rice and solid foods such as lasagne.	Boost thawing. Simmering sauces, casseroles and soups. Cooking and reheating solid foods such as cottage pie. Some puddings and cakes. Cooking critical ingredients, such as eggs, cream or cheese.	Reheating foods. General cooking of small quantities of foods. Some puddings and cakes.	General cooking of fish, vegetables, fruits, tender cuts of meat, poultry and sauces without cream or eggs.

To Cover or Not To Cover

When you want to retain moisture (e.g. in casseroles, steamed sponge pudding) cover with a lid, a plate or pierced cling film. When keeping in the moisture would spoil the dish (e.g. fruit crumble, bread) leave uncovered. If you can't decide, it probably doesn't matter anyway!

Covering food may prevent some sensors from operating properly. If your microwave cooker has a sensor, check with your instruction book to see if cling film should be used (or indeed if food should be covered at all).

6
BREAKFASTS

BREAKFAST HINTS

Fresh Coffee
Fresh coffee prepared by the percolator or filter methods need not be kept warm for hours. Simply reheat individual cups in the microwave. One cup or mug takes 1½–2 minutes on HIGH (100%). Stir before, half way through, and after heating.

Instant Coffee
Microwave a cup or mug of water on HIGH (100%) until just boiling (1½–2 minutes), stirring once during heating. Stir well, then add the coffee powder or granules.

Tea
Microwave a cup or mug of water on HIGH (100%) until just boiling (1½–2 minutes), stirring once during heating. Add a tea bag and allow to stand until the required strength is reached. Remove tea bag.

Milk
Warm milk for drinking or for adding to cereals. Microwave on HIGH (100%) in a cup or dish, stirring once or twice during heating. 150ml/¼ pt milk takes about about 1½ minutes.

Orange and Grapefruit Juice
Thaw frozen concentrated orange or grapefruit juice. Remove any metal from the carton and microwave on MEDIUM–LOW (30%). A 178ml carton takes 2–3 minutes followed by 3–5 minutes standing time.

For freshly squeezed juices, warm whole oranges and grapefruits (or limes or lemons) on HIGH (100%). This way they will yield more juice. Take care with the timing – over-heating will cause the fruit to burst.

1 orange takes about 15–30 seconds on HIGH (100%).
2 oranges take about 45 seconds on HIGH (100%).
3 oranges take about 1 minute on HIGH (100%).

Croissants
Timing is crucial when warming croissants. They can easily turn out soggy!

1 croissant takes about 15 seconds on HIGH (100%).
2 croissants take about 20–25 seconds on HIGH (100%).
3 croissants take about 30 seconds on HIGH (100%).
4 croissants take about 35–40 seconds on HIGH (100%).

Toast
This cannot be made in the microwave.

Fried Bread
If you have a browning dish, pre-heat it on HIGH (100%) according to the manufacturer's instructions. Butter or oil the surface lightly and, with a spatula, press each side of the bread on to the browning dish for a few seconds.

A crispy alternative to fried bread is made in the following way. Melt about 50g/2 oz butter in a small bowl on HIGH (100%) for about 1 minute. Brush this over one side of small bread slices. Arrange the slices, buttered side up, on a roasting rack. Microwave on HIGH (100%) for 3–5 minutes, rearranging them half way through cooking, until dry and firm. As they cool, the slices will crispen.

Bread
Warm fresh bread or freshen stale bread. Microwave whole loaves, slices, or rolls on MEDIUM (50%) until warmed through.

Butter
Soften butter for spreading. 100g/4 oz takes about 30 seconds on MEDIUM-LOW (30%).

Baked Beans
Always cover these or they may splatter the oven walls. One portion takes about 1 minute on HIGH (100%). (See Baked Beans on Toast on page 34.)

Eggs
Eggs can be scrambled, poached, baked and fried in the microwave. (See the individual methods on the following pages.) Timing is crucial and practice makes perfect. The yolks of eggs should always be pricked to prevent them from bursting open. Do not attempt to cook a whole egg in its shell – the build-up of steam inside the shell makes it explode, even after the microwaves have been switched off.

RECIPES FOR BREAKFAST IN MINUTES

Bacon, Egg and Tomato

Method A
1. Cook the bacon under the grill so that the plates can be warmed at the same time.
2. Meanwhile cook the tomato halves on HIGH (100%) until soft. Two halves take about ½–¾ minute. Add ¼ minute for each extra tomato.
3. Break the eggs into individual dishes or ramekins and pierce the yolks (to prevent them bursting). Cover and cook on MEDIUM (50%) for about 1 minute for 1 egg, or 1½ minutes for 2 eggs. Allow to stand for a minute.
4. Meanwhile, reheat the tomatoes and bacon on HIGH (100%) if necessary for ½–1 minute. Serve immediately.

Method B
1. Place the bacon on a roasting rack and cook on HIGH (100%). Two rashers take about 2 minutes, 4 rashers about 3–4 minutes.
2. Meanwhile, heat the plates by immersing them in a bowl of hot water.
3. Cook the tomatoes and eggs as in Method A.
4. Arrange the cooked bacon and tomatoes on the dried plates and, while the eggs are standing, reheat on HIGH (100%) for 1 minute if necessary.

Method C: using a browning dish
1. Pre-heat the browning dish on HIGH (100%) according to the manufacturer's instructions. Brush it lightly with oil.
2. Press the rashers of bacon on to the dish for 10 seconds using a spatula. Turn them over and press down for another 10 seconds.
3. Break the eggs into the dish alongside the bacon, pierce the yolks and cook on HIGH (100%) (about 1½ minutes for 2 rashers of bacon and 2 eggs).
4. Allow to stand for about 1 minute until the eggs are set.
5. Meanwhile, cook the tomato halves in a separate dish (see Method A). Heat the plates in a bowl of hot water.

Baked Beans on Toast

Method A
1. Prepare toast using the grill (warming the plates at the same time) or toaster (warm the plates in a bowl of hot water).
2. Place a slice of hot, buttered toast on a warm plate and spoon over 45ml (3 tbsp) baked beans.
3. Cover and cook on HIGH (100%) for 1 minute or until hot.

Method B
When preparing beans on toast for more than one person, I prefer to cook the beans in a covered container on HIGH (100%), stirring occasionally, until warmed through. Then simply spoon them on to slices of hot, buttered toast.

Eggs: Baked

1. Break an egg into a small dish or ramekin. Prick the yolk.
2. Cover and cook on MEDIUM (50%) until almost set:
    1 egg takes about 1 minute
    2 eggs take about 1½ minutes
    3 eggs take about 2 minutes
    4 eggs take about 2½ minutes.
3. Allow to stand for a minute before serving.

Eggs: Fried

The characteristic appearance and flavour of fried eggs can only be achieved when using a browning dish.
1. Pre-heat the dish according to manufacturer's instructions. If you are cooking bacon on the browning dish too, there will probably be sufficient fat in which to cook the egg (see Method C opposite). Otherwise, lightly butter or oil the surface of the browning dish and crack an egg on to it. The heat will brown the base of the egg.
2. Prick the yolk and complete the cooking on MEDIUM (50%) for about 1 minute.

Eggs: Poached

1. Microwave 150ml/¼ pt water on HIGH (100%) until it just boils. Add a pinch of salt and a dash of vinegar.
2. Break an egg into the water and prick its yolk.
3. Cover and cook on HIGH (100%) for ½–1 minute.
4. Stand for 1–2 minutes until set then use a draining spoon to lift it out.

Eggs: Scrambled on Toast

Serves 1

1 bread slice
butter to taste
2 eggs
30ml (2 tbsp) milk
15g (½ oz) butter
salt and freshly ground pepper

Method
1. Toast the bread slice and keep it hot so that the eggs can be served immediately they are cooked. If using a grill, warm a plate at the same time. If using a toaster, warm a plate in a bowl of hot water. Butter the toast.
2. Beat together the eggs and milk and add the butter.
3. Cook on HIGH (100%) for about 1½ minutes, stirring as soon as the egg sets around the edges of the dish. Continue cooking, stirring frequently, until the eggs are still slightly wet.
4. Stir, season with salt and pepper and serve on the hot toast.

Fish Fingers

Fish fingers do not crisp and brown in the microwave, unless you use a browning dish.

Using a browning dish
1. Pre-heat the browning dish according to the manufacturer's instructions. Spread with a little butter or oil.
2. Place the fish fingers on one half of the hot surface to brown quickly. Turn them over on to the other half.
3. Cook on HIGH (100%): 2 take ¾–1 minute
4 take about 1½ minutes.

Kedgeree

Serves 4–6

2 eggs
450g (1 lb) smoked haddock
225g (8 oz) long grain rice
600ml (1 pt) boiling water
15ml (1 tbsp) chopped parsley
25g (1 oz) butter
salt and freshly ground black pepper

Method
1. *Either* crack the eggs into suitable, small dishes. Prick their yolks, cover and cook on MEDIUM (50%) for 1½–2 minutes. Allow the eggs to cool before chopping them into small cubes.
   Or hard-boil the eggs in a pan on the hob, then shell and chop them when cold.
2. Cook the haddock, covered, on HIGH (100%) for about 6 minutes. Allow to stand for 5 minutes.
3. Meanwhile, put the rice into a deep container, pour the boiling water over, and cook on HIGH (100%) for 10 minutes. Cover and allow to stand for 5 minutes until any remaining liquid has been absorbed and the rice is tender.
4. Flake the fish, discarding skin and bones, and mix it with the rice, eggs, parsley, butter and seasoning to taste.
5. Reheat on HIGH (100%) for 2–3 minutes before serving.

Handy hint: Prepare and refrigerate this dish the day before for simple reheating in the morning.

Porridge

Serves 2

50g (2 oz) quick-cooking porridge oats
300ml (½ pt) water or milk
salt, sugar or honey to taste

Method
1. Mix together the porridge oats and cold water or milk in a deep bowl.
2. Cook on HIGH (100%) for about 4 minutes until thick, stirring frequently.
3. Add salt, sugar or honey and allow to stand for about 3 minutes before serving.

7

SNACKS AND LUNCHES

Your microwave is invaluable for preparing quick snacks at any time of the day. Speedy lunches for one or for several people are also no longer a chore.

HINTS FOR SNACKS AND LUNCHES

Bacon
This makes a quick and tasty snack, particularly in a sandwich. Cook bacon rashers on HIGH (100%) on a roasting rack or a plate. Alternatively, use a browning dish. The longer the cooking time the crisper the bacon becomes. Adjust the cooking times to suit personal preference – see page 34.

Beefburgers/Hamburgers

Beefburgers can be cooked in the microwave, though they will only brown if you use a browning dish. The recipe for Meatballs on page 57 may be prepared with beef, pork or lamb and shaped into burgers.

Method A

Arrange the burgers in a circle on a roasting rack in a large, shallow dish. Cover with absorbent paper to prevent splashing and to soak up fat. Four 100g/4 oz burgers take about 6–8 minutes on HIGH (100%). Turn over once during cooking. Make sure they are cooked through.

Method B: using a browning dish

Pre-heat the dish according to the manufacturer's instructions and sear the burgers on both sides. Cover with absorbent paper and finish cooking them on HIGH (100%). Four 100g/4 oz burgers take 5–6 minutes. Make sure they are cooked through.

Frozen beefburgers can be cooked from frozen, following methods A or B above. Always make sure they are cooked throughout.

> 1 takes about 2 minutes on HIGH (100%)
> 2 take about 4 minutes on HIGH (100%)
> 3 take about 5 minutes on HIGH (100%)
> 4 take about 6 minutes on HIGH (100%).

Bread: Garlic or Herb

Soften butter in the microwave (page 33) and mix with crushed garlic cloves, garlic powder or garlic purée, or chopped fresh or dried herbs. Spread this in a small French stick or Viennese loaf which has been sliced almost through to the base. Wrap the bread in absorbent paper and cook on MEDIUM (50%) until the butter has melted into the bread.

Bread: Crispy Garlic or Herb Slices

Melt flavoured butter (see above) in the microwave and brush this over one side of quartered bread slices. Arrange them (butter side up) on a roasting rack. Cook on HIGH (100%), re-arranging once or twice, until they are dry and firm. The slices will crisp up as they cool.

Cheese

Cheese melts evenly in the microwave – on toast (see page 50) or simply on a plate to be served with crusty bread and pickle. Take care not to over-heat cheese or it will become stringy and tough. Grate it to help it melt quickly and evenly.

Chips

Ordinary chips *cannot* be deep fried in the microwave. However, par-cooking them in the microwave first does speed up the frying time and produces crisper chips. Place the cut potatoes into a container with a little water (60ml/ 4 tbsp to 450g/1 lb potatoes). Cover and cook on HIGH (100%) for about 5 minutes, stirring once or twice. The potatoes should be hot. Drain them, dry them and deep fry immediately as normal.

Chips: oven

Oven chips can be bought for microwave cooking – in a specially-designed container which helps them to brown and crisp.

Ordinary oven chips (not in microwave containers) are reasonably successful when cooked in a browning dish from frozen.

Using a browning dish

Pre-heat the browning dish on HIGH (100%) according to the manufacturer's instructions. Spread the frozen oven chips in one layer over the dish. Cook uncovered on HIGH (100%), 225g/8 oz take about 6–7 minutes. Allow them to stand for 2–3 minutes before serving.

Croûtons

These make a soup into a filling meal. They are easily prepared in the microwave. Thinly butter some bread slices, remove the crusts and cut the slices into small shapes. Spread these over a large plate and cook, uncovered, on HIGH (100%), gently stirring occasionally until they begin to crisp. Two slices take about 2 minutes. They will go on crisping up as they cool.

Eggs

Eggs can be baked, fried, poached and scrambled in the microwave and details can be found in the Breakfasts chapter (pages 35–36). Remember that eggs in their shells must not be cooked in the microwave. The build-up of steam inside causes them to explode.

Omelettes

Microwave-cooked omelettes have a creamy texture. Melt a knob of butter in a 20cm/8 in shallow dish and spread it over the base. Add the beaten eggs and cook on HIGH (100%), lifting the edges from the side of the dish after 1 minute so that the liquid egg runs under the cooked portions. Continue this process until the egg is almost set. Two eggs take 2–3 minutes on HIGH (100%). Add any filling before the omelette is completely set to make sure it is warmed through.

If you are cooking omelettes for more than one or two people, it is more convenient to cook them on the hob, in the conventional way.

Pancakes

Pancakes cannot be cooked successfully in the microwave but they do reheat very well. I keep a stock of pre-cooked pancakes in the freezer, interleaved with greaseproof paper or non-stick paper. Fill the thawed pancakes and simply reheat in the microwave just before serving.

Pasta

Pasta should be cooked in plenty of boiling water in a

large, deep container. You will need to break up long shapes like spaghetti. Place 225g/8 oz pasta in the container and pour over 1.2 litres/2 pints boiling water (from the kettle). Add salt and stir well. Cook uncovered on HIGH (100%) for 7–9 minutes, stirring occasionally, or until the pasta is almost cooked. Allow to stand for 5 minutes before draining and serving. The pasta should still have a slight bite (*al dente*).

Pasta reheats well in the microwave too, either in a sauce or alone. Simply cover and cook on HIGH (100%) for 2–4 minutes for the cooked quantity above. Stir gently once if possible. Adding a little oil or melted butter before reheating helps to separate the pasta shapes.

Pâté

Pâté can be adapted for cooking in the microwave. When a recipe calls for liver or meat to be cooked (with or without fat) before mincing, do this in the microwave in a covered container on HIGH (100%). Once the ingredients have been mixed together and shaped into a circular or loaf-shaped container, the pâté is best cooked on MEDIUM (50%). Always cover the container during cooking to keep in the moisture. A 450g/1 lb container of pâté takes about 15–20 minutes on MEDIUM (50%). After the first 10 minutes of cooking allow it to stand for 5 minutes before continuing.

To make fish pâté, cook kippers or mackerel in the microwave, then flake (discarding skin and bones) and mix with Greek yoghurt or cream cheese, herbs and seasoning.

Pizza

Though you may prefer to cook the base conventionally, pizza dough can be cooked in the microwave. If using a bread dough, press it into greased plates, add a topping and cook uncovered on HIGH (100%). A small individual pizza takes 5–6 minutes: a large one takes about 8 minutes.

If using a scone dough, place on greased plates as above and cook uncovered on HIGH (100%) for 4–5½ minutes for each small pizza. A large pizza takes 6–7 minutes on HIGH (100%).

Use a browning dish if possible to ensure that the pizza browns and crisps on its underside.

Frozen pizzas are convenient. They are best heated from frozen in a pre-heated browning dish. Cook, uncovered, on HIGH (100%) until heated through (5–7 minutes for a 20–23cm/8–9 in pizza).

Make a quick pizza topping. Cook a chopped onion with crushed garlic on HIGH (100%) for 3 minutes. Add a can of chopped tomatoes, some tomato purée and dried herbs. Cook, uncovered, on HIGH (100%) for 5–10 minutes, stirring occasionally, until thick.

Potatoes in their Jackets
Prick washed, dried potatoes with a fork to prevent them from bursting. Stand them in a circle in the microwave. They should not touch each other or the oven walls. Cook, uncovered on HIGH (100%), turning them over half way through cooking and taking out each potato as soon as it is cooked. Cooking times will depend on the size, type and age of potato, but here is a rough guide for potatoes, each weighing about 175g/6 oz:

> 1 takes 5–6 minutes on HIGH (100%)
> 2 take 8–10 minutes on HIGH (100%)
> 3 take 9–12 minutes on HIGH (100%)
> 4 take 10–15 minutes on HIGH (100%).

Potatoes with Cheese and Onion: Split open a cooked potato, add a knob of butter and top with grated cheese and chopped spring onions.

Potatoes with Tomato Sauce: Split open a cooked potato, and top with tomato sauce (recipe on page 105).

Potatoes with Meat Sauce: Top a split cooked potato with the Savoury Minced Beef on page 48.

Potatoes with Chilli: Add chilli powder (to taste) to the Savoury Minced Beef recipe on page 48 and top the cooked potatoes.

Quiches
Best results are obtained if the pastry is cooked conventionally and the filling cooked in the microwave (though I have included instructions for microwave-cooking a pastry flan case on page 133). Cook the filled pastry case on MEDIUM (50%) or MEDIUM–HIGH (70–75%) until the egg is just set. Heating the egg mixture (until slightly set) before pouring it into the pastry case helps the filling set quickly with less chance of making the pastry soggy.

Rice (for savoury dishes)
Rice grains are light, fluffy and separate when cooked in the microwave. Wash the rice and place it in a large, deep container. Pour on *boiling* water (600ml/1 pt for 225g/8 oz rice). Stir well and cook, uncovered, on HIGH (100%) until the rice has absorbed almost all the water (the remainder will be absorbed during the standing time).

225g/8 oz long grain rice takes about 10 minutes on HIGH (100%)

225g/8 oz brown rice takes 15–20 minutes on HIGH (100%) (add an extra 150ml/¼ pt boiling water).

Allow a standing time of 5 minutes before stirring, seasoning and serving.

Sandwiches 'Toasted'
Use a browning dish for 'toasted' sandwiches. Prepare the sandwiches with the buttered sides to the outside. Preheat the browning dish according to the manufacturer's instructions. Press the sandwich on to the hot dish and cook on HIGH (100%) for 30 seconds. Turn the sandwich over on to a fresh (hot) area of the browning dish and cook on HIGH (100%) for a further 30 seconds.

Sausages
There is no doubt that sausages are best cooked conventionally. Sausages cooked by microwaves do not look cooked – they do not have that characteristic brown appearance, and they can easily over-cook. However, better results are obtained with a browning dish. Cooking times will depend on their type and size, but here is a guide for medium sausages:

    2 sausages take 3–4 minutes on HIGH (100%)
    4 sausages take 5–6 minutes on HIGH (100%)
    6 sausages take 9–10 minutes on HIGH (100%).

Sausages cook quite successfully in a sauce or in a casserole. They are moist and tasty and the lack of crispy brown skin is less noticeable.

Soufflés
These are not successful in the microwave. Soufflés need external heat in order to set the crust which traditionally supports the soft, light centre. A soufflé will rise in the microwave but will sink as soon as the power is switched off.

Soups
Most soups can be cooked in the microwave. Generally, reduce the liquid in conventional recipes by about one quarter when cooking in the microwave, as there usually is less evaporation. If the soup is too thick, you can always add extra liquid during cooking.

Use a container which is large enough to hold the soup without it boiling over – particularly important when cooking soup which contains milk. Stir the soup occasionally to ensure even cooking.

Cook on HIGH (100%) unless the soup contains meat which needs tenderising – in which case cook on MEDIUM (50%). Use the ingredient with the longest cooking time as a guide to overall cooking too. Season after cooking.

Soften vegetables in a covered, deep container (with a little butter or cooking oil if liked). Add hot stock (boiling water from the kettle saves time and fuel if more than 600m/1 pt is needed), other ingredients and flavourings. Cover and cook on HIGH (100%) for 15–20 minutes.

Dried Soups: Blend the soup mix with hot water (using the quantity given on the packet). Cook on HIGH (100%) for 4–6 minutes, stirring occasionally. Stand for 5–10 minutes.

Canned Soups: Dilute according to the label instructions and cook on HIGH (100%) for 2–5 minutes.

Remember, always decant soup from cartons because packaging may consist of metal or waxed paper which should not be put in a microwave.

Vegetables: dried
Dried vegetables, such as peas, beans and lentils, re-hydrate well in the microwave but they take a long time. After soaking them for several hours (lentils do not need soaking), cover with boiling water or stock and bring to the boil on HIGH (100%). Continue cooking on MEDIUM (50%) or MEDIUM-LOW (30%) until tender, stirring occasionally.

RECIPES FOR SNACKS AND LUNCHES

Bacon, Lettuce and Tomato Sandwich

Serves 1

2 lean streaky bacon rashers, rinds removed
2 bread slices
15–30ml (1–2 tbsp) mayonnaise
lettuce leaves
tomato slices

Method
1. Put the bacon rashers on a roasting rack or plate.
2. Cook on HIGH (100%) for 1½–2 minutes (or longer if you want the bacon really crisp). Allow it to stand for a minute. *Alternatively*, brown the bacon on a pre-heated browning dish.
3. Spread the bread slices with mayonnaise and arrange some lettuce leaves and sliced tomato on one piece.
4. Top with the crispy bacon and the other bread slice.

Handy hint: If you use a browning dish to cook the bacon, you may prefer to 'toast' the sandwich in the browning dish too.

Baked Beans on Toast: See page 34.

Beef: Savoury Minced (Bolognese)

Serves 4

15ml (1 tbsp) oil
1 large onion, chopped
100g (4 oz) lean streaky bacon, chopped
2 medium carrots, chopped
450g (1 lb) lean minced beef
150ml (¼ pt) beef stock *or*
　400g can tomatoes
30ml (2 tbsp) tomato purée
15ml (1 tbsp) fresh chopped herbs *or*
　5ml (1 tsp) dried herbs
1–2 garlic cloves, crushed
salt and freshly ground black pepper

Method
1. Put the oil, onion, bacon and carrots in a large container. Cover and cook on HIGH (100%) for 5 minutes, stirring once.

2. Stir in the minced beef, breaking it up with a fork. Cover and cook on HIGH (100%) for 5 minutes, stirring once or twice.
3. Drain off juices and skim off any excess fat if wished. Return the meat juices to the meat.
4. Stir in the stock or tomatoes with the remaining ingredients.
5. Cover and cook on HIGH (100%) for 15–20 minutes, stirring once or twice.

Handy hints: Use this recipe as a base for Shepherd's/ Cottage Pie (page 62), for Lasagne (page 55), as a Bolognese Sauce (thicken with a little cornflour mixed with stock or red wine) or as a Chilli Sauce (add chilli powder to taste).

Cauliflower Cheese with Savoury Bread Rolls

Serves 4

450g (1 lb) cauliflower florets
60ml (4 tbsp) water
50g (2 oz) butter or margarine
50g (2 oz) flour
600ml (1 pt) milk
salt and freshly ground black pepper
50g (2 oz) cheese, grated
4 bread rolls
butter
crushed garlic, chopped herbs, dried herbs or lemon juice

Method A
Cauliflower
1. Put the cauliflower and water in a large container. Cover and cook on HIGH (100%) for 5–7 minutes, stirring once or twice, until just cooked. Drain well.

Sauce
1. Meanwhile, prepare the sauce. Melt the butter or margarine in a jug on HIGH (100%) for about 1 minute.
2. Stir in the flour then gradually add the milk, whisking continuously.
3. Cook uncovered on HIGH (100%) for 6–7 minutes, whisking frequently.
4. Season to taste and stir in the cheese.
5. Pour the sauce over the cauliflower.
6. Either reheat on HIGH (100%) for 2–3 minutes or brown under the grill (make sure the container is suitable).

Bread rolls
1. Mix together some butter (softened in the microwave – see page 33) with crushed garlic, chopped fresh herbs, dried herbs or lemon juice.
2. Split the rolls and spread them with the flavoured butter.
3. Arrange the rolls in a circle on absorbent paper.
4. Cook on MEDIUM (50%) for about 1 minute or until the butter has melted in the bread.

Method B
1. Cook the cauliflower in a saucepan on the hob for 10–15 minutes.
2. Meanwhile, prepare the sauce in the microwave oven as in Method A.
3. While the sauce is standing, warm the bread rolls as in Method A.

Cheese on Toast

Serves 1

Toast a slice of bread, spread it with butter and top with cheese slices. Cook on HIGH (100%) for about 30 seconds or until the cheese has melted.

Cheese Pudding

Serves 4

225g (8 oz) breadcrumbs
225g (8 oz) mature Cheddar cheese, grated
600ml (1 pt) milk
40g (1½ oz) butter
3 eggs (size 2), beaten
pinch of mustard powder
salt and freshly ground black pepper

Method
1. Mix the breadcrumbs with 175g/6 oz grated cheese and put them in a buttered 1.1 litre/2 pt soufflé dish.
2. Mix together the milk, butter, eggs, mustard powder, salt and pepper and cook on HIGH (100%) for 1–2 minutes until the butter melts.
3. Pour the mixture over the breadcrumbs.
4. Sprinkle the remaining 50g/2 oz cheese over the top. Cook on MEDIUM-LOW (30%) for 15–20 minutes, or until the pudding is set, turning the dish occasionally. The pudding is cooked when a knife inserted in the centre comes out clean.

Eggs Florentine

Serves 4

1 quantity of white sauce (page 103)
450g (1 lb) spinach, washed
salt and freshly ground black pepper
knob of butter
4 eggs, poached (page 35)

Method
1. Prepare the white sauce as described on page 103.
2. Cook the spinach with just the water clinging to its

leaves, covered, on HIGH (100%) for about 5 minutes or until just tender. Drain, season to taste and stir in butter.
3. Arrange the poached eggs on the bed of spinach.
4. Pour the white sauce over the eggs to coat them.
5. If necessary reheat the dish on HIGH (100%) for about 1 minute.

Fish Cakes

Serves 4

450g (1 lb) potatoes, sliced
60ml (4 tbsp) water
450g (1 lb) fish fillets, such as cod, haddock, etc.
butter
1 egg, beaten
salt and freshly ground black pepper
15–30ml (1–2 tbsp) chopped parsley or other fresh herbs
fresh breadcrumbs, toasted breadcrumbs (page 130) or
    crushed cornflakes

Method
1. Cook the potatoes with the water, covered, on HIGH (100%) for 5–8 minutes, stirring occasionally. Leave to stand for 5 minutes.
2. Meanwhile, cook the fish, dotted with butter and covered, on HIGH (100%) for 3–5 minutes or until it flakes when tested with a fork.
3. Flake the fish, discarding any skin and bones. Mash the potatoes.
4. Mix together the potatoes and fish with the remaining ingredients. Shape into four cakes and chill until firm.
5. Coat with fresh breadcrumbs if cooking in a frying pan or under the grill. Coat with toasted breadcrumbs (see page 130) or crushed cornflakes if cooking in the microwave.

6. *Either* cook in a frying pan or under the grill, *or* place on a roasting rack, cover with absorbent paper, and cook on HIGH (100%) for 3–4 minutes. Leave them to stand for 2 minutes before serving.

Fish Florentine

Serves 4

½ quantity of white sauce (page 103)
450g (1 lb) spinach
salt and freshly ground black pepper
butter
4 fish fillets, such as cod, haddock, smoked haddock, etc.

Method
1. Prepare the white sauce as described on page 103.
2. Wash the spinach, shaking off the excess water. Cover and cook on HIGH (100%) for about 5 minutes, stirring once, or until just tender. Drain, season, and stir in a knob of butter if liked.
3. Place the fish in a shallow container, dot with butter, cover and cook on HIGH (100%) for 3–6 minutes or until the fish flakes when tested with a fork.
4. Arrange the fish on top of the spinach and pour the white sauce over.
5. Reheat on HIGH (100%) if necessary for about 1 minute before serving.

Fish Pie

Serves 4

450g (1lb) potatoes, sliced
60ml (4 tbsp) water
450g (1 lb) white or smoked fish
butter
1 quantity of white sauce (page 103)
30ml (2 tbsp) chopped parsley
2–4 hard-boiled or baked eggs (page 35), chopped
salt and freshly ground black pepper
toasted breadcrumbs (optional), page 130

Method
1. Cook the potato with the water, covered, on HIGH (100%) for 5–8 minutes, stirring occasionally. Leave to stand for 5 minutes.
2. Meanwhile, put the fish in a shallow container, dot with butter, cover and cook on HIGH (100%) for 3–6 minutes or until the fish flakes when tested with a fork.
3. Flake the fish, discarding any skin and bones.
4. Mix together the white sauce, parsley, eggs and fish. Season to taste and arrange in a pie dish.
5. Mash the potato and spoon it over the fish mixture.
6. Reheat the dish, uncovered, on HIGH (100%) for 3–5 minutes before serving. Top with toasted breadcrumbs for an attractive finish. Alternatively, brown the surface under a hot grill if the container is suitable.

Fish Pudding

Follow the recipe for Cheese Pudding on page 51. Replace the cheese with 225–350g/8–12 oz fish (cod, smoked haddock) which has been cooked, covered, on HIGH (100%) for 2–3 minutes or until the fish flakes when tested with a fork. Flake the fish, discarding any skin and bones. Add seasoning such as dill or parsley if liked.

Lasagne

Serves 4–5

For best results, and if time allows, make up the lasagne and let it stand for several hours or overnight (covered in the refrigerator).

1 quantity of savoury minced beef (page 48)
175g (6 oz) 'no pre-cook' or fresh lasagne sheets
1 quantity of white sauce (page 103)
50g (2 oz) cheese, grated

Method
1. Using a flameproof dish measuring about 25.5cm × 20.5cm/10 × 8 in, arrange layers of the meat, lasagne and sauce, finishing with a layer of sauce. (If time allows, cover and refrigerate for several hours or overnight.)
2. Sprinkle the cheese over the top and cook on MEDIUM (50%) for about 30 minutes or until the pasta is tender.
3. Brown under a hot grill before serving.

Macaroni Cheese

Serves 4

225g (8 oz) macaroni
900ml (1½ pt) water, boiling
40g (1½ oz) butter
40g (1½ oz) flour
400ml (¾ pt) milk
salt and freshly ground black pepper
2.5ml (½ tsp) mustard powder
50–100g (2–4 oz) cheese, grated
toasted breadcrumbs (optional), page 130

Method

1. *Either* cook the macaroni on the hob (according to packet instructions) while you prepare the sauce. *Or* place the macaroni in a large, deep container and pour over the boiling water. Cook, uncovered, on HIGH (100%) for about 8 minutes, stirring once, until just tender. Allow it to stand while you prepare the sauce.
2. Melt the butter on HIGH (100%) for about 45 seconds. Stir in the flour, then gradually add the milk, whisking well.
3. Cook on HIGH (100%) for 5–6 minutes, whisking frequently until thickened and boiling. Season to taste and add the mustard and cheese.
4. Drain the macaroni and stir this into the sauce.
5. *Either* reheat in a serving dish on HIGH (100%) for 2–3 minutes, and top with toasted breadcrumbs (optional, but gives an attractive finish). *Or* use a flameproof serving dish and brown the surface under a hot grill.

Meat Loaf

Your favourite meat loaf recipes can be cooked in the microwave. Combine all the ingredients in the usual way and press the mixture into a greased loaf dish. Cover with microwave or greaseproof paper and cook on MEDIUM (50%). A loaf containing 450g/1 lb raw minced meat will take about 20 minutes. When it is cooked, the loaf should be shrinking away from the sides of the dish. Use a microwave thermometer for accuracy, if wished.

Handy hints: A loaf shape tends to dry out at the corners. Protecting these areas with a little foil helps the loaf cook more evenly – but check with your instruction book on the use of foil first. Alternatively, why not cook the loaf in a different shape? A ring mould gives excellent results – cooking is quick and even and the finished loaf is easy to slice.

Meatballs

Makes 20

450g (1 lb) minced beef, lamb or pork
50g (2 oz) breadcrumbs
15–30ml (1–2 tbsp) tomato purée
1 small onion, chopped
fresh or dried mixed herbs, to taste
salt and freshly ground black pepper
1 egg, beaten

Method
1. Mix together all the ingredients and shape the mixture into 20 balls.
2. Arrange them in one layer in a large, shallow container. Cover and cook on MEDIUM (50%) for 15–20 minutes, repositioning the meatballs once or twice during cooking.
3. Leave to stand for 3–5 minutes before serving.

Serving suggestion: These are delicious with tomato sauce (see page 105). Pour the sauce over the meatballs after the first 10 minutes cooking. Cover and cook on MEDIUM (50%) for a further 10–15 minutes, stirring gently once or twice.

Mushrooms with Garlic

Serves 4

25–50g (1–2 oz) butter
1–2 garlic cloves, crushed
225g (8 oz) button mushrooms
salt and freshly ground black pepper
30ml (2 tbsp) chopped parsley

Method
1. Put the butter and garlic into a container, cover and cook on HIGH (100%) for 1 minute.
2. Stir in the mushrooms to coat them with butter.
3. Cover and cook on HIGH (100%) for 3–4 minutes, stirring once.
4. Season to taste and stir in the parsley just before serving.

Serving suggestion: Serve with toast, croûtons (see page 42) or crusty French bread.

Pasta with Tomato Sauce

Serves 4

1 quantity of tomato sauce (page 105)
275g (10 oz) pasta shapes such as shells, twists, quills or bows
1.1 litre (2 pt) water, boiling
5ml (1 tsp) oil
salt and freshly ground black papper

Method A
1. Prepare the sauce.
2. Place the pasta shapes in a large, deep container and pour the boiling water over. Add the oil and stir well. Cook, uncovered, on HIGH (100%) for about 10 minutes or until just tender, stirring occasionally.
3. Leave to stand for 5 minutes before draining.
4. Season to taste and pour the tomato sauce over.
5. Reheat on HIGH (100%) for 2–3 minutes before serving.

Method B
Prepare the pasta on the hob, following packet instructions while the tomato sauce is cooked in the microwave as above.

Serving hints: While the pasta and sauce are cooking, prepare a crunchy, green salad or some garlic bread (page 40) to serve with it.

Potatoes in their Jackets: See page 44.

Potato Pie

This is a substantial dish, particularly if grated cheese is added between the layers.

1. In a buttered flameproof dish, arrange alternate layers of thinly sliced potatoes and finely sliced onions. Season each layer with salt and pepper to taste.
2. Pour over sufficient milk (or cream and milk) to come almost to the top of the potatoes.
3. Dot with butter, cover and cook on MEDIUM (50%) until the potatoes are tender (about 20–25 minutes for 450g/1 lb potatoes and 175g/6 oz onions). Leave to stand for 5–10 minutes.
4. Sprinkle with breadcrumbs and/or grated cheese and brown under a hot grill.

Potato Salad

1. Cook potatoes in their jackets on HIGH (100%). See page 44 for a guide to cooking times.
2. Cool the potatoes before skinning them (if preferred) and cutting into cubes.
3. Mix with mayonnaise (or a mixture of mayonnaise and yoghurt), chopped onion and seasonings to taste, until the potatoes are well-coated.

Potato Soup with Leeks

Serves 4–6

2 medium leeks, thinly sliced
1 small onion, finely chopped
25g (1 oz) butter
350g (12 oz) potatoes, thinly sliced
600ml (1 pt) chicken stock, boiling
salt and freshly ground black pepper
pinch of grated nutmeg
150ml (¼ pt) double cream
30ml (2 tbsp) chopped chives

Method
1. Put the leeks, onion and butter into a large container, cover and cook on HIGH (100%) for 5 minutes, stirring once.
2. Add the potatoes, *boiling* stock, seasoning and nutmeg. Cover and cook on HIGH (100%) for about 10 minutes, stirring once or twice, until the vegetables are tender.
3. Tip the mixture into a food processor and purée until smooth. Stir in the cream.
4. Serve topped with chives.

Quiche or Savoury Flan

Serves 4–6

20.5cm (8 in) shortcrust pastry flan case
3 eggs
300ml (½ pt) milk or milk and cream mixed
4 lean streaky bacon rashers, chopped
1 small onion, chopped
salt and freshly ground black pepper
50g (2 oz) cheese, grated

Method
1. *Either* cook the pastry case in the microwave following directions on page 133.
   Or bake the pastry case in the conventional way. This produces better results. Remember to bake the case in a microwave-safe dish.
2. Mix the remaining ingredients and pour into the pastry case.
3. Cook, uncovered, on MEDIUM (50%) for about 15 minutes or until almost set. The filling should finish setting if the flan is allowed to stand for 10–15 minutes.

You may find better results are obtained if you start cooking the filling in the microwave (until it just begins to thicken) before pouring it into the pastry case. Then complete the cooking on MEDIUM (50%) until just set.

Handy hint: Since better results are achieved with conventionally-cooked pastry cases, why not batch cook them for the freezer? Take one out when needed to fill and finish off in the microwave. See page 132. Alternatively, buy a pre-cooked savoury pastry case.

Reheating hint: Ready-cooked flans can be reheated in the microwave. Take care not to over-heat them or the pastry will become soggy. A flan which serves 4–6 takes 4–5 minutes on MEDIUM (50%).

Rice: Savoury with Mushroom Sauce

Method A
1. Cook the rice in the microwave with some turmeric and/or herbs. Follow the guidelines on page 45.
2. Prepare a quantity of Mushroom Sauce using the method on page 103. Serve with the rice.

Method B
Prepare the sauce on the hob while the rice cooks in the microwave. This will save time.

Shepherd's/Cottage Pie

Serves 4

1. Prepare a quantity of Savoury Minced Beef (page 48), adding your favourite herbs and flavourings.
2. Cook sliced potatoes with a little water in a covered container on HIGH (100%) until tender, stirring once or twice (450g/1 lb potatoes and 60ml/4 tbsp water take 6–8 minutes). Allow them to stand for 5 minutes.
3. Drain and mash the potatoes with salt, pepper, butter and a little milk.
4. Spoon the potato over the mince in a flameproof dish.
5. Reheat on MEDIUM (50%) for about 10 minutes. Brown the surface under a hot grill, or sprinkle with toasted breadcrumbs (page 130).

Soup: Bortsch

Serves 4–6

1 large beetroot, grated
1 medium carrot, grated
1 medium onion, grated or finely chopped
2 celery sticks, finely chopped
30ml (2 tbsp) tomato purée
600ml plus (1 pt plus) beef stock
25g (1 oz) butter
30ml (2 tbsp) lemon juice
1 bay leaf
5ml (1 tsp) sugar
soured cream

Method
1. Mix together all the ingredients (except the cream) in a large container. Cover and cook on HIGH (100%) for 15–18 minutes, stirring two or three times.
2. Allow the soup to stand for 5 minutes before discarding the bay leaf. Add extra stock if it is needed to thin the soup.
3. Serve hot, garnished with a swirl of soured cream.

Serving suggestion: If serving the soup chilled – omit the butter or replace it with oil.

Soup: Tomato and Onion Cup

Serves 1

2.5ml (½ tsp) cornflour
½ chicken stock cube
1 tomato, chopped
3 spring onions, chopped
salt and freshly ground black pepper
chopped fresh herbs or dried herbs
milk or water

Method
1. Place the cornflour and crumbled stock cube in a large mug and stir in the tomato, onions, seasoning and herbs to taste. Half fill the mug with milk or water (not too full or the mug will overflow during cooking – you can always top up with extra milk or water after cooking).
2. Cover and cook on HIGH (100%) for about 3 minutes, stirring once or twice.
3. Allow the soup to stand for 3 minutes before stirring and serving.

Serving suggestion: Serve simply with crusty fresh bread. Alternatively, keep a supply of croûtons in a sealed container for serving on occasions like this. (See page 42.)

Soup: Vegetable

Serves 4–6

2 lean streaky bacon rashers, chopped
1 small onion, finely chopped
1 medium leek, finely chopped
3 celery sticks, finely chopped
3 medium carrots, finely chopped
1 medium potato, finely chopped
30ml (2 tbsp) cornflour
1 litre (1¾ pt) beef or chicken stock, boiling
30ml (2 tbsp) tomato purée
2.5ml (½ tsp) mixed dried herbs
salt and freshly ground black pepper

Method

1. Put the bacon and vegetables in a large container. Cover and cook on HIGH (100%) for 10 minutes, stirring once or twice.
2. Stir in the cornflour, then gradually add the boiling stock.
3. Add the remaining ingredients, cover and cook on HIGH (100%) for 10–15 minutes, stirring occasionally.
4. Allow the soup to stand for 5 minutes before adjusting the seasoning and adding extra stock or water to thin the soup if necessary.

Serving suggestion: For a creamed soup, purée the mixture and stir in a 150ml carton of single cream.

Welsh Rarebit

Serves 1

1 bread slice
75g (3 oz) Cheddar or Caerphilly cheese, grated
10ml (2 tsp) beer
knob of butter
salt and freshly ground black pepper
mustard powder

Method
1. Toast the bread slice.
2. Mix together the cheese, beer, butter, seasoning and mustard powder to taste.
3. Cook, uncovered, on HIGH (100%) for 30 seconds or until the cheese mixture is hot and bubbling, stirring once.
4. Pour the cheese over the toast and serve.

8
MAIN MEALS

This chapter gives advice and hints on preparing a variety of meat, fish and vegetable dishes which can make up part or all of a substantial meal.

GETTING IT TOGETHER

A main meal provides an occasion when all your planning, preparation and co-ordination culminate in a delicious spread. It seems appropriate therefore, at this stage in the book, to talk about planning, preparation and co-ordination. Together with making the best use of your microwave alongside your other cooking appliances, the prospect can sound daunting. You may ask yourself how you can possibly 'get it together' and serve the meal on time. Perhaps my most important piece of advice would be to start slowly and advance gently. We all know that 'practice makes perfect' and that it takes a while to achieve it. Begin by preparing one or two simple items of a meal in the microwave – the vegetables perhaps. Then go on to simple recipes – basic ones from your instruction book which have been designed specifically for your microwave cooker. As your confidence grows, you will want to cook your own recipes in the microwave. Pages 20–27 give numerous hints on adapting your own conventional recipes for microwave cooking.

Ironically perhaps, you will not save time by attempting to cook *everything* in the microwave. So when time is short, prepare one dish in the microwave while cooking another on the hob, or under the grill. In other words, make the best use of your 'kitchen team'.

Here are some ideas for getting together three simple meals, a roast dinner or Sunday lunch and, the high spot of culinary entertaining, Christmas dinner. Each of them is designed to use your microwave as part of the 'team' – with the hob, grill and conventional oven each playing its part. All the dishes and foods mentioned are to be found in the pages of this book.

By cooking in advance and by making use of long standing times and the speedy reheating facility of your microwave cooker, you will be able to plan menus, automatically using the microwave.

Spaghetti Bolognese and Stewed Fruit

Cook the Bolognese sauce in the microwave. Then, while the fruit is cooking in the microwave, boil the spaghetti on the hob. If the fruit is to be accompanied by custard, cook this in the microwave first while the spaghetti cooks on the hob, then the fruit can cook in the microwave while the first course is being eaten. Pages 48, 42, 106 and 108.

Poached Fish and Vegetables and Fruit Crumble

Prepare the pudding first, microwaving the fruit and then the topping. Either microwave the vegetables and arrange on a covered dish to reheat before serving, or cook some or all of the vegetables on the hob while the pudding is in the microwave. Cook the fish just before serving it. The pudding can be reheated just before serving. Pages 74 and 108.

Meat Loaf with Jacket Potatoes and Salad and Jam Sponge Pudding

Wash and prick the potatoes. While they cook in the microwave, prepare the meat loaf. Wrap the cooked potatoes tightly in foil. They will keep hot for at least 20 minutes. While the meat loaf cooks in the microwave, assemble the salad. Allow the loaf to stand. Microwave the sponge pudding and allow to stand. Serve the savoury course, reheating the potatoes briefly if necessary. If the pudding has cooled too much by the time it is served, simply reheat whole or in portions. Pages 44, 56 and 121.

A word about cheese and wine

Cheese can be 'ripened' or brought quickly to room temperature in the microwave. Take care not to over-heat it though – this is best done on LOW (10%).

Take the chill off red wine: open the bottle, return its cork, heat on HIGH (100%) for 15 seconds then decant.

Roast Dinner/Sunday Lunch

It is always a good idea to prepare the starter and the dessert in advance – preferably the day before. Choose a pudding which is served cold, and a starter which can be reheated (such as soup) or which can be assembled quickly before serving (such as melon, grapefruit, pâté or prawn cocktail).

1. In the morning prepare and cook the vegetables separately in the microwave until just tender. Save any juices for the gravy. Arrange the vegetables on a serving dish, cover and keep them in a cool place.
2. Weigh the meat and calculate the cooking time on MEDIUM (50%), according to how well done you prefer meat. Add to this 20–30 minutes standing time. At the specified time – usually 1–1¾ hours before serving, depending on the weight of the meat – begin cooking the joint following the guidelines on page 79. A microwave thermometer is helpful for cooking meat accurately, to your personal taste. When the correct temperature (page 80) has been reached, remove the joint from the oven and cover securely with foil. Allow to stand for 20 minutes. (The joint will stay hot for 30–40 minutes.)
3. Use the time while the meat is cooking to prepare or assemble starters and/or desserts.
4. While the joint is being carved (by someone else, hopefully!) microwave the gravy, using the vegetable

and meat juices (page 105).

5. Just before serving, reheat the dish of vegetables on HIGH (100%) for 3–4 minutes or until hot throughout.

A useful tip

When family or friends stay for the weekend and plans for a Sunday-morning outing are made, I like to be included too. So I cook the joint in advance, sometimes the day before. (It is easier to carve cold and can be kept ready, sliced and wrapped in the refrigerator.) Then on the day, I microwave the vegetables early, as explained above. I simply make the gravy while the whole meal reheats.

Christmas Dinner

1. *The day before*

   Prepare the stuffing using the microwave to soften the onions (page 71).

   You will probably have cooked the pudding, either by microwave or conventionally, several weeks earlier. However, do not despair if you have not. A perfectly acceptable Christmas pudding can be cooked in the microwave the day before. Add a little extra colouring such as treacle or gravy browning, and flavouring such as spices, lemon rind and orange rind (page 108).

   Microwave the bread sauce (page 104) or cranberry sauce (page 104) to save time on the day.

2. *Early on Christmas Day*

   Microwave the potatoes until just cooked (these are now ready for roasting). Microwave the vegetables, one type at a time, and arrange them on one or more serving platters. Small quantities of many different vegetables are a real treat and involve the use of only one cooking container. Save the cooking juices for gravy. Cover the vegetables and store them in a cool place.

3. Microwave a sweet sauce to accompany the pudding and cover with wet grease-proof paper.

4. Prepare the turkey. Weigh it and calculate the cooking time at 6–8 minutes per 450g/1 lb. Add an extra 30 minutes to allow for standing time. Brush the breast with melted, unsalted butter. Wrap foil around the narrow parts of the wings and legs to prevent them drying out – check with your manufacturer's instruction book regarding the use of foil. Place the turkey inside a large roasting bag (or slit one to make it large enough to cover the turkey and tuck underneath), tie loosely and place, breast side down, on a roasting rack in a large container. Make sure no parts touch the cavity wall during cooking. At the calculated time, microwave the turkey for half the cooking time. See the roasting chart on page 80.

5. While the turkey is cooking, you could prepare a cold starter.

6. Turn the bird over, breast side up. Protect the breast bone with a strip of foil. Cook for the remaining time. Fifteen minutes before the end, drain off all the juices. Finish cooking and wrap the turkey with foil and allow to stand for 30–50 minutes.

7. Meanwhile, roast the microwave-cooked potatoes in a very hot conventional oven. Crisp some bacon rashers and sausages at the same time. If a crisp skin is preferred on the turkey, allow the standing time to take place in the hot oven – remove the foil before putting in the oven.

8. Make the gravy in the microwave (page 105).

9. *Finally*
    Reheat the vegetables in the microwave and warm the plates in the conventional oven or in a bowl of hot water while the turkey is being carved (hopefully, by someone else!) and the cold starter is being eaten.

10. Reheat the sweet sauce (on LOW/10% if possible) while the main course is being eaten. Lastly, reheat the pudding, whole or in individual portions, just before serving (page 108).

Stuffing: Parsley and Lemon

Serves 4–6

1 medium onion, finely chopped
25g (1 oz) butter
50g (2 oz) mushrooms, chopped (optional)
100g (4 oz) fresh breadcrumbs
1 egg, beaten
30ml (2 tbsp) chopped parsley
grated rind and juice of ½ lemon
salt and freshly ground black pepper

Method
1. Put the onion in a container, cover and cook on HIGH (100%) for 3 minutes.
2. Stir in the butter until it melts, then mix in the remaining ingredients.
3. Use to stuff poultry, meat or fish. Alternatively, cook on HIGH (100%) for 1–2 minutes and serve separately.

Stuffing: Sage and Onion

Serves 4–6

2 large onions, finely chopped
25g (1 oz) butter
100g (4 oz) fresh breadcrumbs
10ml (2 tsp) dried sage
1 egg
salt and freshly ground black pepper

Method
As for Parsley and Lemon.

Serve with poultry or pork.

FISH

Fish stays beautifully whole during microwave cooking. The texture and flavour are rather special too. The fish is cooked very quickly, in the least amount of liquid so that all the flavour is sealed in.

HINTS FOR MICROWAVING FISH

Microwaving is particularly suitable for fish recipes which call for poaching. The quantity of liquid needed can be reduced. Use only as much as you will need to make a sauce. When no sauce is required, cook the fish just as it is.

When cooking whole fish, overlap the tails or the thin ends. This produces an even layer of fish which is more likely to cook evenly. Alternatively, wrap the tails in foil to protect them from the microwaves. (Check with your instruction book on the use of foil in your particular model.)

If the skin is left on whole fish during cooking – slit it in one or two places to allow steam to escape and to prevent it bursting.

Add salt *after* cooking, otherwise it tends to dry out the surface of the fish.

Butter or fat can be added if liked to enhance the flavour. Melt it and brush it over the fish for best results.

Always cover fish during cooking to keep in the juices.

Turn the container once or twice during cooking in microwaves without turntables.

Stir seafood and quick-cooking ingredients into a dish towards the end of the cooking period.

Fish is cooked when the flakes separate easily when eased apart with a fork.

When a brown finish is required on fish, use a browning dish pre-heated according to manufacturer's instructions.

Fish cooked in a sauce is best cooked on MEDIUM (50%), again to encourage even cooking.

Breadcrumbed or battered fish is not successful in the microwave. It will be soggy, not crisp. Fish fingers are successful on a browning dish – turn to page 36 for details of how to cook them.

Microwave and roasting bags and 'boil-in-the' bags are useful for cooking fish (see page 24). Remember to tie them loosely to allow steam to escape.

Thawing fish fillets is only necessary if you have to carry out extra preparation such as skinning or adding bread-crumbs or batter. For 450g/1 lb fish fillets allow about 3–4 minutes on DEFROST (30%), followed by a defrosting–standing time of 5 minutes, 2–3 minutes more on DEFROST (30%) and a further standing time of 5 minutes. Where no preparation is needed, fillets may be cooked from frozen. The cooking time will of course be longer, so check the fish often to avoid over-cooking of thinner areas.

Whole fish needs thawing before cooking, otherwise the thinner areas will over-cook while thicker areas remain frozen. See your instruction book for times in your particular microwave.

Fish Cooking Time Guide
Cook fish, covered, on HIGH (100%).
  Whole fish: 4–6 minutes per 450g/1 lb
  Fillets and steaks: 2–3 minutes (thick)
                    1–2 minutes (thin).
Allow a standing time of 5 minutes.

If you find that fish over-cooks (or spatters) on HIGH (100%), reduce the power level to MEDIUM (50%) and cook for a little longer. Test in the usual way – the fish should flake when tested with a fork.

RECIPES

Fish: Poached

1. Arrange the fish in a shallow container.
2. Add 30–45ml/2–3 tbsp water, fruit juice, milk, stock or wine.
3. Brush with melted butter if wished, season with pepper and add slices of lemon.
4. Cover and cook on HIGH (100%) for 1–3 minutes for fillets, 2–4 minutes for thick cutlets or rolled fillets, 4–6 minutes for whole fish, or 4–6 minutes per 450g/1 lb for larger fish.
5. Allow a standing time of 5 minutes. Season with salt. Serve with a sauce such as Parsley (recipe on page 103) or Hollandaise (opposite).

Hint: When cooking more than one whole fish, reposition them half way through cooking. Large whole fish (1.4kg/ 3 lb or more) should be turned over half way through cooking.

Hollandaise Sauce

Usually a difficult, time-consuming sauce to make, hollandaise is quickly prepared in the microwave.

100g (4 oz) butter
30ml (2 tbsp) white wine vinegar
2 egg yolks
salt and freshly ground black pepper

Method
1. Cut the butter into small pieces and put in a bowl. Cook on HIGH (100%) for ½–1 minute until just melted (the butter must not be too hot).
2. Add the vinegar, egg yolks and a little seasoning.
3. Whisk the mixture well.
4. Cook on HIGH (100%), whisking every 10–15 seconds until the sauce is thick and creamy. Take care not to over-cook or the sauce will curdle.
5. Serve warm with poached fish, particularly salmon.

Fish: Stuffed

Serves 2

two 175g/6 oz whole fish such as trout
salt and freshly ground black pepper
1 quantity of stuffing, such as Parsley and Lemon (page 71)
25g (1 oz) butter

Method
1. Wash, dry and lightly season the fish cavities with salt and pepper and fill them with the stuffing mixture. Slit the skin in two or three places.
2. Arrange the fish on a plate with their tails overlapping.
3. Melt the butter on HIGH (100%) for 45 seconds and brush it over the fish.

4. Cover and cook on HIGH (100%) for 4–6 minutes or until the fish flakes when tested with a fork.
5. Allow a standing time of 5 minutes before serving.

Trout with Almonds

Serves 4

four 175g/6 oz trout
salt and freshly ground black pepper
lemon slices
25–50g (1–2 oz) butter, melted
toasted almonds (page 129)

Method
1. Wash, dry and lightly season the cavities of the fish. Put a few lemon slices inside each fish.
2. Slit the skins in two or three places.
3. Arrange the fish around the outer edge of a large plate, overlapping the tail ends to produce a more even layer.
4. Brush with melted butter, cover and cook on HIGH (100%) for 6–8 minutes. Allow the fish to stand for 5 minutes, then sprinkle over some toasted almonds.

Handy hint: You may find that fish cooks more evenly and spatters less when cooked on MEDIUM (50%). There is less chance of over-cooking it too. Remember to lengthen the cooking time – by one third to one half.

MEAT AND POULTRY

Microwave cooking is a very clean method of cooking meat and poultry. Other advantages include speedy cooking, good flavour retention and, usually, less shrinkage. Of course, we all know that meat joints and whole poultry will not have the brown crisp exterior of their conventionally roasted equivalents. However, there are many ways of overcoming this comparatively small problem. Large joints do, in fact, brown naturally to some degree and using roasting bags helps this process tremendously (roasting bags also help to keep the cavity – particularly in a combination cooker – clean). Turn to page 23 *et seq.* for more information on browning.

Use your microwave to thaw meat and poultry too. Check with your manufacturer's instruction book for methods and times. Always make sure that meat is *completely* thawed before cooking, allowing the recommended defrosting-standing time.

GENERAL HINTS FOR COOKING MEAT

Choose even-shaped pieces of meat to encourage even cooking.

Prevent over-cooking of thin areas of joints or wing-tips etc. of poultry by covering them with small pieces of foil. Your instruction book will give you guidance for your particular model.

Arrange smaller pieces of meat, like chops, with the thicker areas towards the outside of the container.

Minced meat can be shaped into balls, burgers or ring moulds to encourage it to cook evenly.

Cover meat and poultry during cooking to prevent splashes on the cavity wall and to keep moisture in.

Secure meat with string or wooden (not metal) skewers.

Boiling joints, such as bacon, are ideal for microwave cooking, but instead of immersing the joint in water, it is cooked in a roasting bag. (See page 81.)

Braising and Pot Roasting can be done in the microwave (see page 86) by making use of low power levels. Beef cuts such as topside and silverside need tenderising in liquid. In fact, less liquid is needed in the microwave since there is less evaporation. Consequently the meat juices are concentrated and very tasty. Braising and pot roasting should be completed on MEDIUM (50%) or MEDIUM-LOW (30%) in a covered container.

Casseroles and Stews generally need a little less liquid since there is less evaporation. Cut meat into even-sized pieces. Browning the meat before adding the other ingredients improves both the flavour and the finished appearance of a casserole. Brown the meat quickly in a frying pan on the hob before adding it to the casserole. The less tender cuts of meat which are used for casseroles are best microwaved on MEDIUM-LOW (30%) or MEDIUM

(50%) (after an initial period on HIGH (100%) to heat up all the ingredients) to imitate the long, slow cooking of conventional casseroling. It is also worth remembering that you can develop the flavour even further by cooking the casserole one day and reheating it the next.

Frying and Grilling. Meats such as steaks, chops and beefburgers are best microwaved using a browning dish to sear and brown them. I must say though, that I still prefer them cooked in the conventional way – grilled or fried.

Pies with a raw meat filling cannot be cooked in the microwave. However, cooked pies can be reheated (see pages 83 and 133). Save time by preparing pie fillings in the microwave for topping with pastry and cooking in the conventional oven.

Roasting joints (particularly those without a bone) are best cooked in a roasting bag, or in a roasting rack and covered with a split roasting bag. The meat should not sit in its own juices. A microwave thermometer (see page 14) is an excellent investment if you plan to cook meat joints in the microwave. You can cook the meat to perfection – cooking beef so that its centre is still pink is simple and works every time. Overleaf is a useful guide to internal temperatures of cooked meat and their approximate cooking times. The chart includes cooking times on HIGH (100%), but if time is available you may prefer the results of meat cooked on MEDIUM (50%).

Turn meat joints over, half way through cooking.

Allow a standing time of 15 minutes or more after cooking to allow the temperature of the meat to even out and to make carving easier. Cover it with foil during this standing time. Make use of this time by cooking vegetables or making gravy in the microwave.

Turn to page 88 for the general method for roasting chicken.

Roasting Chart

Meat	Remove from microwave at about	Approximate temperature after standing	Approximate cooking time per 450g/1 lb on HIGH (100%)
Beef, rare	49°C/120°F	60°C/140°F	5–6 minutes
medium	60°C/140°F	71°C/160°F	6–7 minutes
well done	71°C/160°F	77°C/170°F	8–9 minutes
Lamb, medium	66°C/150°F	77°C/170°F	8–9 minutes
well done	71°C/160°F	82°C/180°F	9–10 minutes
Pork and bacon, well done	82°C/180°F	88°C/190°F	9–10 minutes
Veal	66°C/150°F	77°C/170°F	8–10 minutes
Chicken	82°C/180°F	88°C/190°F	8–10 minutes
Turkey	79°C/175°F	90°C/195°F	9–11 minutes

Roly Poly Puddings

Filled with bacon, chicken or Savoury Minced Beef (page 48), these savoury puddings cook well in the microwave. They should be wrapped in non-stick or greased grease-proof paper – loosely to allow the pudding to rise. Twist the 'Christmas cracker' ends to close them. Cook on MEDIUM (50%) for about 15 minutes. Allow a standing time of 5 minutes before testing by inserting a skewer. If it comes out clean, the pudding is cooked. If not, cook on MEDIUM (50%) for a further 2–3 minutes before allowing it to stand again.

Suet Puddings

Suet puddings cook quickly in the microwave, eliminating the traditional steamy kitchen associated with cooking suet crust pastry. You may find that the pudding lid hardens slightly, particularly at the edges. Cook the filling (such as steak and kidney or bacon) before adding it to the pastry, to give a soft, moist result. The filled pudding should be covered and cooked on HIGH (100%). A 1.1 litre/2 pt pudding takes about 10 minutes. Allow a standing time of 5 minutes. If the pastry is not quite cooked (test it by easing an area open with a fork), cook for 1–2 minutes before standing the pudding again.

RECIPES

Bacon: 'Boiled'

1. Put the bacon joint in a large container and cover with boiling water. Allow to stand for 10 minutes, then discard the water. This removes some of the saltiness.
2. Put the bacon joint in a roasting bag and tie loosely to allow the steam to escape. Sit the joint on a roasting rack.
3. Cook on HIGH (100%) or MEDIUM (50%), turning the joint over half way through cooking. A 1.4kg/3 lb joint of bacon takes 30–35 minutes on HIGH (100%) or 35–45 minutes on MEDIUM (50%). If using a microwave

thermometer, see page 80 for a guide to the internal temperatures of cooked meat.
4. Allow a standing time of 15 minutes before carving.

Beef Olives

The appearance of this dish is improved if a browning dish is used to colour the meat after stage 1. Alternatively, brown in a frying pan before microwave cooking.

Serves 4

½ quantity of parsley and lemon stuffing (page 71)
4 thin slices of beef topside
600ml (1 pt) beef stock, boiling
salt and freshly ground black pepper
30ml (2 tbsp) chopped parsley
cornflour

Method

1. Spread the stuffing over the slices of topside and roll them up. Secure with string or thread.
2. Arrange the beef rolls in a shallow container and pour round sufficient boiling stock to come half way up their sides.
3. Cover and cook on MEDIUM (50%) for about 1 hour or until the meat is just tender. The cooking time will depend on the thickness of the beef. Turn the beef rolls over once or twice during cooking.
4. Allow a standing time of 10–15 minutes before removing the meat from the stock.
5. Season the gravy with salt and pepper and stir in the parsley.
6. Thicken the gravy by mixing a little cornflour with a little cold water and stirring this into the stock. Cook on HIGH (100%) until boiling, stirring frequently.
7. Serve the meat with the gravy.

Beef Pie

Prepare the fillings in the microwave – such as Savoury Minced Beef (page 48) or Beef in Red Wine (below) or Beef Stew (overleaf). When converting your own recipes, use less liquid than normal and if necessary add extra thickening towards the end of cooking. To do this, mix some flour or cornflour with a little cold stock, water or wine to make a smooth paste. Add a little of the hot liquid from the meat and stir. Return this mixture to the meat and stir well. Cook on HIGH (100%) for 1–2 minutes to cook the flour.

Top the meat with a pastry crust and cook the pie in the conventional oven. Unless you have a combination cooker, results in the microwave are not acceptable – the filling bubbles over and the pastry does not crisp or brown. Save time by cooking a large quantity of filling in the microwave and freezing it in pie-size portions. Why not cook a batch of pastry circles or shapes to fit your favourite dish? Freeze them ready for topping a hot pie filling at a moment's notice. Pies can be reheated in the microwave but take care not to overcook them or the pastry becomes soggy.

Beef in Red Wine (or Beef Bourgignon or Burgundy Beef)

Serves 4

175g (6 oz) onions, chopped
1–2 garlic cloves
100g (4 oz) lean streaky bacon, chopped
15ml (1 tbsp) oil
700g (1½ lb) braising steak, cubed
**30ml (2 tbsp) flour, seasoned with salt and freshly ground
   black pepper**
1 bouquet garni
300ml (½ pt) red wine
100g (4 oz) button mushrooms

Method
1. Put the onions, garlic, bacon and oil into a large container, cover and cook on HIGH (100%) for 3 minutes.
2. Toss the beef in the seasoned flour – this is most easily done in a polythene bag. Stir the meat into the onion mixture.
3. Add the bouquet garni and red wine.
4. Cover and cook on HIGH (100%) for 10 minutes or until boiling.
5. Continue cooking on MEDIUM (50%) for about 50 minutes or until the meat is tender, stirring once or twice during cooking.
6. Stir in the mushrooms and cook on HIGH (100%) for 2–3 minutes.
7. Allow a standing time of 5–10 minutes before serving.

Beef Stew

Serves 4

1 medium onion, chopped
450g (1 lb) vegetables such as carrots, leeks, celery, turnip, parsnip, swede, chopped
15ml (1 tbsp) oil
450g (1 lb) braising steak, cubed
30ml (2 tbsp) flour
15ml (1 tbsp) dried mixed herbs
300ml (½ pt) beef stock, hot
10ml (2 tsp) mustard powder
30ml (2 tbsp) tomato purée

Method
1. Put the onion, vegetables and oil into a large container. Cover and cook on HIGH (100%) for 5 minutes, stirring once.
2. Add the braising steak and cook on HIGH (100%) for 5 minutes, stirring once.
3. Stir in the flour, then add the remaining ingredients.

4. Cover and cook on MEDIUM (50%) or MEDIUM-LOW (30%) for about 1 hour or until the beef is tender, stirring two or three times during cooking.
5. Allow a standing time of 10 minutes before serving.

Beef Stew with Herb Dumplings

Serves 4

Ingredients as for Beef Stew, opposite

Dumplings:
225g (8 oz) self-raising flour
5ml (1 tsp) salt
100g (4 oz) shredded suet
5ml (1 tsp) dried mixed herbs

Method
1. Prepare the beef stew as described in the recipe opposite.
2. When the meat is just tender, prepare the dumplings. Sieve together the flour and salt and stir in the suet and herbs if used. Mix with cold water to form a stiff dough. Shape the dough into 8–12 dumplings.
3. Add the dumplings to the cooked stew for the final 10 minutes of cooking.

Handy hint: Try making Lemon and Herb Dumplings – just add the finely grated rind of one lemon with the herbs. Cheese Dumplings are good too – push a small cube of cheese into the centre of each dumpling and pinch the edges together to seal it.

Bolognese Sauce

Use the recipe for Savoury Minced Beef, page 48.

Braised Beef or Pot Roast

Topside and silverside are most suitable.

1. Put the meat in a large, deep container and pour in 300–600ml/½–1 pt hot stock.
2. Cover and cook on HIGH (100%) until the stock boils.
3. Continue cooking on MEDIUM (50%) for 25–30 minutes per 450g/1 lb, or on MEDIUM-LOW (30%) for 40 minutes per 450g/1 lb. If time allows, the slower cooking produces better results. Half way through cooking, turn the joint over and add diced or sliced vegetables such as carrot, onion, leek, celery and mushrooms. If possible, use a microwave thermometer to tell you when the centre of the meat is cooked. See the chart on page 80 for temperatures.
4. Allow a standing time of 15 minutes before serving.

Chicken Casserole

Use the recipe for Beef Stew, replacing the beef with 4 chicken portions at stage 2, and the beef stock with chicken stock at stage 3 (page 84).

4. Cover and cook on HIGH (100%) for 20–25 minutes or until the chicken is tender. Stir once or twice during cooking.
5. Allow a standing time of 5–10 minutes before serving.

Chicken Chasseur

Serves 4

4 chicken portions
25g (1 oz) butter
4 spring onions, chopped
**25g (1 oz) flour, seasoned with salt and freshly ground
black pepper**
300ml (½ pt) chicken stock, hot
150ml (¼ pt) white wine
100g (4 oz) button mushrooms
15ml (1 tbsp) chopped parsley

Method

1. Put the chicken portions in a large container. Cover and cook on HIGH (100%) for 10 minutes, turning them half way through cooking.
2. In another container, cook the butter and onions on HIGH (100%) for 1–2 minutes.
3. Stir the seasoned flour into the onions and gradually add the hot stock, stirring continuously.
4. Add the remaining ingredients.
5. Pour the sauce over the chicken, cover and cook on HIGH (100%) for 15 minutes or until the chicken is tender. Turn the chicken once during cooking.
6. Allow a standing time of 10 minutes.

Chicken Curry

Serves 4

4 chicken portions

Sauce:
15ml (1 tbsp) oil
225g (8 oz) onions, finely chopped
30ml (2 tbsp) cornflour
1–2 garlic cloves, crushed
30–45ml (2–3 tbsp) curry paste
400g can tomatoes
300ml (½ pt) chicken stock
30ml (2 tbsp) lemon juice
5ml (1 tsp) sugar
salt and freshly ground black pepper

Method

1. Put the chicken in a large container. Cover and cook on HIGH (100%) for 10 minutes, turning once during cooking.
2. In another container, cook the oil and onions on HIGH (100%) for 3 minutes.

3. Stir in the cornflour then add the remaining ingredients, stirring well.
4. Pour the mixture over the chicken, cover and cook on HIGH (100%) for 15 minutes or until the chicken is tender. Turn the chicken over half way through cooking.
5. Allow a standing time of 10 minutes before serving with rice (see page 45).

Chicken: 'Roast'

1. Wash and dry the chicken well.
2. Brush with melted butter. If liked, add a little soy sauce, yeast extract, paprika or brown sauce to the butter – this gives a rich colour to an otherwise pale chicken and adds flavour too. Season with pepper (not salt).
3. Place the chicken in a roasting bag, breast side down, on a roasting rack in a large, shallow container. Tie the bag loosely (use string or thread) to allow steam to escape.
4. Cook the chicken, turning it over half way through. Cook for 7–9 minutes per 450g/1 lb on HIGH (100%) or
    10–12 minutes per 450g/1 lb on MEDIUM (50%).
Allow a standing time of 15–20 minutes, covered loosely with foil.

Important: Always make sure chicken is thoroughly cooked. Test by inserting a skewer or knife into the thickest part of the inside thigh. The juice of cooked chicken should run clear.

If using a microwave thermometer, place this in the same thick part of the thigh. Remove the chicken from the microwave when the thermometer reads 82°C/180°F. This will rise to about 88°C/190°F during the standing time.

Handy hint: Orange and lemon peel, herbs, garlic or bacon rinds placed in the chicken cavity add delicate flavours to the cooked meat.

Curried Meat

Serves 4–6

1. Prepare a curry sauce as in stages 2 and 3 of Chicken Curry (page 87).
2. Stir in 700g/1½ lb lean braising beef, stewing lamb or pork, cut into cubes.
3. Cover and cook on HIGH (100%) for 5 minutes or until boiling.
4. Continue cooking on MEDIUM (50%) for 40–50 minutes or until the meat is tender. Pork usually tenderises more quickly than lamb, and lamb more quickly than braising beef.
5. Allow a standing time of 10 minutes before serving with rice (page 45).

Gammon with Pineapple

Serves 4

1. Trim the rind off 4 gammon steaks (about 175g/6 oz each) and snip into the fat to prevent the steaks from curling up during cooking.
2. Cook on a roasting rack on HIGH (100%) for about 10 minutes until tender. Turn the steaks over half way through cooking.
3. Place a drained pineapple ring on each slice and cook on HIGH (100%) for 1 minute before serving.

Handy hint: A browning dish gives a good finish to the gammon steaks. Pre-heat the dish according to the manufacturer's instructions. After searing the gammon steaks on both sides, cook on HIGH (100%) for 6–8 minutes, then for 1 minute with the pineapple added.

Heart

Recipes using heart need careful cooking in the micro-wave – it will tenderise sufficiently if cooked in plenty of liquid or sauce. Cook on HIGH (100%) until boiling, then continue cooking on DEFROST (30%) for at least 1 hour, until the heart is tender.

Kidneys in Sauce

As with conventional cooking, care is needed not to over-cook the kidneys or they will toughen.

Serves 4

25g (1 oz) butter
8 lambs' kidneys, skinned, halved and cored
15ml (1 tbsp) flour
150ml (¼ pt) stock or red wine, or a mixture
salt and freshly ground black pepper
30ml (2 tbsp) chopped parsley

Method
1. Cook the butter on HIGH (100%) for 1 minute until melted and stir in the kidneys.
2. Cover and cook on HIGH (100%) for 6–7 minutes, stirring once or twice.
3. Stir in the flour then gradually add the stock or wine and seasoning.
4. Cover and cook on HIGH (100%) for 2–4 minutes until the sauce thickens, stirring once or twice. Stir in the parsley before serving.

Lamb Casserole

Follow the recipe for Beef Stew on page 84, replacing the beef with lamb and the mixed herbs with rosemary.

Lamb Casserole: Mediterranean Style

Serves 4

1 medium aubergine, sliced
salt and freshly ground black pepper
15ml (1 tbsp) olive oil
1 medium onion, sliced
1 garlic clove, crushed
100g (4 oz) mushrooms, sliced
15g (½ oz) flour
450g (1 lb) lamb fillet, cubed
150ml (¼ pt) lamb or chicken stock
400g can tomatoes
5ml (1 tsp) dried oregano
225g (8 oz) courgettes, thinly sliced

Method

1. Sprinkle the aubergine slices with salt and leave to stand for 30 minutes. Rinse well, drain and dry.
2. Put the oil, onion, garlic and mushrooms in a large container, cover and cook on HIGH (100%) for 5 minutes, stirring once.
3. Stir the flour into the onion mixture, then add the lamb, stock, tomatoes and aubergines. Cover and cook on HIGH (100%) for about 10 minutes, stirring occasionally, or until the mixture boils.
4. Add the oregano and courgettes. Cover and cook on MEDIUM (50%) for about 20 minutes, stirring occasionally, until the lamb and vegetables are tender.

Lamb: Moussaka

Serves 4–6

2 medium aubergines, sliced
salt
1 quantity of tomato sauce (page 105)
350g (12 oz) lamb, minced or chopped finely
1 quantity of white sauce (page 103), using 500ml/¾ pt
   milk
50g (2 oz) cheese, grated
1 egg, beaten

Method
1. Slice the aubergines and sprinkle with salt. This will help remove any bitter taste. After 15 minutes, rinse, drain and dry the slices.
2. Prepare the tomato sauce, adding the lamb at stage 3.
3. Prepare the white sauce, using 500ml/¾ pt milk, and stir in the cheese. Stir in the beaten egg.
4. Arrange the meat sauce and aubergine slices in layers in a flameproof dish and top with the cheese sauce.
5. Cover and cook on MEDIUM (50%) for 20–25 minutes until tender.
6. Brown under a hot grill before serving.

Liver and Bacon

Using a browning dish will improve the finished colour of liver.

Serves 4

450g (1 lb) lambs' liver, thinly sliced
15ml (1 tbsp) flour, seasoned with salt and freshly ground
   black pepper
15g (½ oz) butter
4 lean back bacon rashers

Method

1. Coat the liver with the seasoned flour.
2. Pre-heat a browning dish according to manufacturer's instructions.
3. Melt the butter on the hot surface and add the liver, pressing it down well to brown it. Turn it over.
4. Cook on HIGH (100%) for 2–3 minutes.
5. Add the bacon rashers and cook on HIGH (100%) for about 2 minutes.
6. Cover and allow it to stand for 5 minutes, then check that the liver is cooked to your liking. If necessary, cook for a further ½–1 minute and stand again.

Liver and Bacon with Gravy

Serves 4

25g (1 oz) butter
1 medium onion, chopped
450g (1 lb) lambs' liver, thinly sliced
15ml (1 tbsp) flour, seasoned with salt and freshly ground
   black pepper
150ml (¼ pt) beef stock, hot
2.5ml (½ tsp) dried sage

Method

1. Cook the butter and onion on HIGH (100%) in a covered container for 3 minutes.
2. Coat the liver in the seasoned flour, then stir it into the onion mixture with the hot stock and sage.
3. Cover and cook on HIGH (100%) for about 10 minutes, stirring occasionally.
4. Allow a standing time of 10 minutes.

Oxtail

Always cook oxtail using conventional methods. It does not tenderise sufficiently in the microwave.

Pork Casserole

Follow the recipe for Beef Stew on page 84, replacing the beef with pork, and the mixed herbs with sage. At stage 4, cook on HIGH (100%) for 5 minutes then switch to MEDIUM (50%) for 30–40 minutes, stirring once or twice. Add a peeled, cored and sliced cooking apple for the final 10 minutes' cooking if wished. Allow a standing time of 10 minutes before serving.

Pork and Vegetable Stir Fry

Serves 4

15ml (1 tbsp) oil
275g (10 oz) pork fillet, cut into thin strips
225g (8 oz) carrots, thinly sliced
225g (8 oz) courgettes, cut into thin strips
1 medium red or yellow pepper, deseeded and sliced
4 spring onions, sliced
425g can baby sweetcorn, drained
100ml (4 fl oz) hoi sin sauce

Method
1. Put the oil into a large container and stir in the pork. Cook, uncovered, on HIGH (100%) for 4–5 minutes, stirring once or twice.
2. Add the carrots and cook, uncovered, on HIGH (100%) for 3 minutes.
3. Stir in the courgettes, pepper, onions and sweetcorn. Cook, uncovered, on HIGH (100%) for 5 minutes, stirring once.
4. Add the sauce and cook on HIGH (100%) for 3–5 minutes until bubbling hot. Stir before serving.

VEGETABLES

Fresh vegetables from the microwave have a lovely colour and flavour and you can cook them to that cooked-yet-crisp stage which is perfect.

HINTS FOR MICROWAVING VEGETABLES
Choose good quality vegetables. Old vegetables can dry out and toughen in the microwave.

Use the minimum amount of water. 45ml/3 tbsp is usually sufficient, though root vegetables or older vegetables may need extra.

Cut or trim vegetables into small, uniform pieces to encourage even cooking.

Prick the skins of whole vegetables such as potatoes, courgettes and tomatoes. This helps prevent them bursting as a result of a steam build-up inside.

Arrange whole vegetables, such as potatoes, in a circle – do not put one in the centre because it will cook only very slowly.

Stir or shake vegetables once or twice during cooking to encourage even cooking. Turn over large items such as whole potatoes half way through cooking.

Season vegetables with salt *after* cooking as salt tends to draw out the moisture and dry the surfaces.

Always cover vegetables during cooking to retain moisture and flavour.

Microwave bags, roasting bags and 'boil-in-the' bags are useful for cooking vegetables. Remember to leave the opening loose to allow steam to escape.

Cook vegetables on HIGH (100%) and allow a 3–5 minutes' standing time before serving.

Different vegetables can be cooked together so long as they have similar cooking times. Check with the cooking chart in your instruction/recipe book. Alternatively, add quick-cooking vegetables towards the end of the cooking period.

Frozen vegetables do not need thawing before cooking.

Blanching vegetables. Small quantities (no more than 450g/1 lb) at a time are suitable. Put the vegetables in a container with 45–60ml/3–4 tbsp water. Cover and cook on HIGH (100%) for 3–4 minutes, stirring half way through, until the vegetables are hot. Drain and tip them into ice-cold water, then drain again and freeze.

RECIPES

Cauliflower with Cheese Sauce

Cauliflower cooks best when cut into florets.

Serves 4
1. Put 450g/1 lb florets into a container with 45ml/3 tbsp water.

2. Cover and cook on HIGH (100%) for about 8 minutes, stirring or shaking twice during cooking.
3. Allow a standing time of 5 minutes.
4. Prepare the cheese sauce as described on page 103.
5. Drain the cauliflower, season to taste and coat with the sauce.
6. If necessary reheat on HIGH (100%) for 1–2 minutes.

Cauliflower Cheese with Savoury Bread Rolls
See the recipe on page 49.

Chestnuts

Shelling chestnuts (to accompany sprouts or to be included in a stuffing) is simple with a microwave. Watch them carefully though – they dry up if they are cooked for too long.
1. Using a sharp knife, cut a cross in the skins (to prevent them exploding).
2. Cook on HIGH (100%) in an uncovered container. 225g/8 oz take about 3 minutes.
3. Remove soft ones and strip off their skins. Cook the remaining chestnuts for a further 30 seconds or until soft enough to peel.

Herbs: Drying

Dry fresh herbs in the microwave and store them in an airtight jar in a dark place.
1. Place washed and dried leaves of fresh herbs, in a single layer, on absorbent paper.
2. Cook, uncovered, on HIGH (100%) for 30 seconds and check them.
3. Continue cooking, uncovered, for 30 second bursts until the herbs are quite dry and will crumble between your fingers. Turn the leaves over and reposition them once or twice during cooking.
4. Allow the herbs to stand for 10 minutes before packing (whole, or crushed) into screw-top jars.

Marrow: Stuffed Rings of

Serves 4

1 quantity of savoury minced beef (page 48)
four 2.5cm/1 in thick marrow rings, deseeded
15ml (1 tbsp) water
salt and freshly ground black pepper
25–50g (1–2 oz) cheese, grated

Method
1. Prepare the Savoury Minced Beef.
2. Arrange the marrow rings in a circle in a shallow dish and sprinkle the water over them.
3. Cover and cook on HIGH (100%) for 6–8 minutes or until just tender.
4. Allow to stand for 5 minutes before draining off the water.
5. Season to taste with salt and pepper.
6. Meanwhile, heat the Savoury Minced Beef on HIGH (100%) for 5–8 minutes until heated through.
7. Pile the beef into the marrow rings and sprinkle the grated cheese over the top.
8. Reheat on HIGH (100%) for 1–2 minutes if necessary.

Variation: Replace the cheese with tomato sauce, recipe on page 105.

Handy hints: Use a flameproof container and brown the finished dish under a hot grill.

Marrow rings are also good filled with a thick white sauce (page 103) into which has been mixed prawns, tuna, cooked chopped ham or chicken, or mushrooms.

Pease Pudding

Serves 4–6

225g (8 oz) split yellow peas
1 small onion, chopped
750ml (1¼ pt) bacon stock, hot
freshly ground black pepper
25g (1 oz) butter

Method
1. Pour plenty of boiling water over the split peas, cover them and allow to stand for ½–1 hour.
2. Drain and put the peas into a large, deep container with the onion, hot bacon stock and pepper.
3. Cover and cook on HIGH (100%) for 20 minutes or until the peas are tender, stirring two or three times during cooking.
4. Remove the cover and boil rapidly on HIGH (100%) until the mixture thickens to the desired consistency, stirring frequently.
5. Stir in the butter before serving.

Peppers – Stuffed

Peppers may be stuffed with your favourite filling. Blanch them in boiling water for 2 minutes first (with the tops and seeds removed).

Serves 4

25g (1 oz) butter
1 large onion, finely chopped
1 celery stick, finely chopped
50g (2 oz) mushrooms, chopped
15ml (1 tbsp) tomato purée
10ml (2 tsp) French mustard
75g (3 oz) cooked rice

continued overleaf

Peppers – Stuffed (contd.)
225g (8 oz) ham, chicken or other cooked meat, minced or finely chopped
15ml (1 tbsp) chopped parsley
salt and freshly ground black pepper
2 peppers, tops removed, deseeded and blanched

Method
1. Cook the butter, onion and celery on HIGH (100%) in a covered container for 3 minutes.
2. Stir in the remaining stuffing ingredients and mix well.
3. Pile the mixture into the peppers and arrange these in a buttered, shallow container. Replace their tops.
4. Cover and cook on HIGH (100%) for 10–12 minutes.
5. Allow to stand for 5 minutes before serving.

Serving suggestion: Serve with tomato sauce, page 105.

Variation: This recipe can also be made using Savoury Minced Beef (page 48) to stuff the peppers.

Potato Chips

Deep frying must never be attempted in the microwave. However, chips will be crisper if par-cooked in the microwave before deep drying on the hob. See page 41.

Potatoes: in their Jackets see page 44.

Potatoes: Mashed

Cook potatoes in their jackets (page 44) and allow them to cool slightly. Peel them and mash with butter, milk and seasoning.

Alternatively, peel and dice potatoes and put into a large container with 60ml/4 tbsp water. Cover and cook on HIGH (100%) for about 10 minutes (for 450g/1 lb) until tender, stirring once or twice. Allow to stand for 5 minutes, drain and mash with butter, milk and seasoning.

Potatoes: Roast

Unless you have a combination oven, potatoes cannot be roasted in the microwave – they will not crisp and brown sufficiently even in a browning dish. However, you can save time and fuel by par-cooking them in the microwave (on HIGH/100% for about 5 minutes) before adding them to the roasting tin. This method produces really crisp potatoes.

SAUCES AND GRAVIES

Sauces and gravies can add flavour, moisture and a contrast in texture to many dishes. Made in the microwave, they do not stick or burn on to their containers like those made in a saucepan on the hob. Small quantities work well too.

HINTS FOR MAKING SAUCES AND GRAVIES
Make sauces and gravies in the serving jug for convenience. Large quantities can be made in a bowl or a large jug. Make sure the container is large enough to hold the sauce without it boiling over. Use one which allows for easy stirring – sauces containing flour or eggs need stirring frequently during cooking to prevent lumps from forming.

It is not worth covering sauces and gravies – they need frequent stirring and a cover would be a hindrance.

If you need to reduce or thicken a sauce, simply cook it uncovered on HIGH (100%), boiling rapidly, until you have the desired quantity. Speed up the process by using a wide-topped container.

As with conventional cooking, save the juices from meat, fish and vegetables to add flavour to sauces and gravies.

To develop the flavour of a sauce or gravy, after it has boiled and thickened, reduce the microwave power to MEDIUM-LOW (30%) and continue cooking for a few minutes extra.

Sauces reheat well in the microwave – heat on HIGH (100%), stirring frequently.

Thawing sauces is simple. Cover the container and cook on DEFROST (30%), breaking up the sauce with a fork as it softens. 600ml/1 pt sauce takes 10–12 minutes.

RECIPES

Basic White Sauce *makes just over 600ml/1 pt*

40g (1½ oz) butter
40g (1½ oz) flour
600ml (1 pt) milk
salt and freshly ground black pepper

Method
1. Put the butter in a bowl or jug. Cook on HIGH (100%) for ½–1 minute until melted.
2. Stir in the flour and gradually blend in the milk. Season to taste.
3. Cook, uncovered, on HIGH (100%) for 5–6 minutes, whisking frequently during cooking.

Handy hint: Heating the milk for 3 minutes on HIGH (100%) before adding it to the flour and butter mixture helps to make a creamy sauce. Having added the hot milk, cook on HIGH (100%) for 2–3 minutes, whisking occasionally.
Parsley Sauce: Add 30–45ml/2–3 tbsp chopped parsley to the cooked sauce.
Cheese Sauce: Add 75g–100g/3–4 oz grated cheese to the cooked sauce.
Mushroom Sauce: At stage 1, cook some chopped mushrooms with the butter, covered, on HIGH (100%) for 2 minutes.
Onion Sauce: At stage 1, cook some chopped onion in the butter, covered, on HIGH (100%) for 3 minutes.
Other Variations: Add prawns, chopped anchovies or chopped hard-boiled eggs to the cooked sauce. Use to fill *vol-au-vents* too.

Apple Sauce

Serve with roast pork.

Cook 225g/8 oz sliced cooking apples on HIGH (100%)

with 15ml/1 tbsp water and 10ml/2 tsp sugar (optional) for about 5 minutes, stirring often, until soft and puréed. Beat in a knob of butter.

Bread Sauce

Serve with chicken or turkey.

1 small onion, sliced
1 bay leaf
6 black peppercorns
2 whole cloves
300ml (½ pt) milk
50–75g (2–3 oz) fresh breadcrumbs
25g (1 oz) butter
salt

Method
1. Put the onion, bay leaf, peppercorns, cloves and milk into a bowl or jug.
2. Cook on HIGH (100%) for 3–5 minutes until boiling. Cover and continue cooking on MEDIUM-LOW (30%) for 10 minutes.
3. Strain and return the milk to the container.
4. Stir in the breadcrumbs and butter, cover and cook on MEDIUM (50%) for 5 minutes, stirring occasionally.
5. Season to taste with salt and stir well.

Cranberry Sauce

Serve with turkey, duck or lamb.

Put 225g/8 oz cranberries in 300ml/½ pt water or orange juice and bring to the boil on HIGH (100%). Continue cooking, uncovered, on HIGH (100%) for about 5 minutes or until the cranberries burst. Sweeten with sugar to taste. Allow the sauce to cool to room temperature for serving.

Tomato Sauce

Serve with fish, vegetables, meat or pasta.

25g (1 oz) butter
1 garlic clove, crushed
1 medium onion, finely chopped
400g can chopped tomatoes
15ml (1 tbsp) tomato purée
dried mixed herbs, to taste
salt and freshly ground black pepper

Method
1. Cook the butter, garlic and onion, covered, on HIGH (100%) for 3 minutes.
2. Stir in the tomatoes, tomato purée, herbs and seasoning.
3. Cover and cook on HIGH (100%) for 5–8 minutes, stirring occasionally.

Handy hint: If a smoother sauce is preferred, blend or sieve the cooked sauce.

Gravy

Make delicious gravy using the juices left over after cooking a joint of meat. Skim off the fat, leaving the juice. Stir in a little flour or cornflour. Gradually stir in stock or cooking liquid from the vegetables. Cook on HIGH (100%) until it boils, stirring two or three times during cooking. To reduce the gravy, or to improve its flavour, continue cooking on MEDIUM (50%) or MEDIUM-LOW (30%). Season to taste with salt and pepper.

Handy hints: If a darker gravy is preferred, stir in a little gravy browning.

9
DESSERTS AND PUDDINGS

Delicious puddings and light desserts provide the finishing touches to a meal. Made in the microwave they are prepared in very little time and can be even more successful than when cooked conventionally.

HINTS FOR DESSERTS AND PUDDINGS

Custards
Custards are simple to make in the microwave – for pouring, for trifles or for creamy cold desserts mixed with fruit or chocolate. Check with your manufacturer's instructions for the best setting on which to cook custards containing eggs. In microwave cooking as well as in conventional cooking, care must be taken not to over-

heat and therefore curdle the mixture. See page 116 for Custard Tart and Baked Egg Custard.

Custard and blancmange powders made up in a jug are cooked in minutes – with no sticky saucepans to wash. Mix the powder with a little milk (according to the packet instructions) to form a smooth paste. Gradually stir in the rest of the milk. Cook on HIGH (100%) (6–7 minutes for 600ml/1 pt) until the custard thickens, stirring frequently during cooking. Sweeten to taste.

Cheesecakes

Most cheesecakes can be cooked in the microwave. Cook on MEDIUM (50%) and stop cooking when the centre still appears slightly undercooked. It will finish cooking during the standing time.

Cold cheesecakes are simple too. The gelatine or chocolate used as the setting agent is prepared as follows:

Gelatine: Heat some of the liquid from the ingredients on HIGH (100%) until it is hot (but not quite boiling). Briskly stir in the gelatine powder. Do not allow the mixture to boil or the gelatine will lose its setting quality. Add this to the main mixture, following the method given in the recipe.

Chocolate: Simply melt chocolate in a bowl in the microwave. Heat on MEDIUM (50%) or MEDIUM-LOW (30%), stirring frequently, until melted. Take care not to over-heat it.

Coconut and nuts: For topping a cheesecake, toast coconut by spreading some desiccated coconut over a large plate and cooking uncovered on HIGH (100%) until golden brown. Watch it carefully and stir or shake the coconut every minute to prevent patchy browning and burning. Alternatively, toast some nuts (see page 129).

Biscuit bases: see page 113.

Christmas Pudding

Your favourite Christmas pudding recipe will cook in a very short time. Take care though – it can easily burn in the microwave.

Soften the dried fruit first by cooking it in liquid, covered, on HIGH (100%) for 10 minutes. Allow it to cool.

When adapting your own recipe, add only 30ml/2 tbsp of alcohol, replacing the rest with milk or fruit juice. Add extra liquid too – about 15ml/1 tbsp per egg.

Use butter in place of suet (chill it and grate it into the pudding mixture).

Cook on MEDIUM (50%) for best results – a 450g/1 lb pudding takes about 15–20 minutes, a 900g/2 lb pudding takes about 25–30 minutes.

Store in a cool place for up to 2–3 weeks.

To reheat puddings, heat on MEDIUM (50%) – 450g/1 lb takes 3–5 minutes, 900g/2 lb takes 8–12 minutes. An individual portion takes about 45 seconds on HIGH (100%).

Crumble Toppings

These are suitable for microwave cooking though they will not brown or crisp. Sprinkle crumble over warm cooked fruit. Cook on HIGH (100%) for 5–7 minutes. Allow a standing time of 5 minutes.

Fruit

Microwaved fruits are juicy and keep their shape beautifully. Their colour and flavour are excellent too since cooking is completed in just a little water and in the shortest possible time. Cook (or cut fruit into) uniform pieces to encourage even cooking. Cover during cooking.

Put the prepared fruit in a container with 45–60ml/3–4 tbsp water (rhubarb and soft fruits such as raspberries need no additional water). Cover and cook on HIGH (100%), stirring occasionally. Cooking times will depend on the type of fruit, its quality, its age, its starting temperature and its preparation (whole or sliced).

As a guide: 450g/1 lb soft fruit takes 2–5 minutes
450g/1 lb hard fruit takes 7–10 minutes

The skins of whole fruits, such as apples, should be split in order to prevent them bursting open during cooking.

Fruits with skins, such as plums, should be sweetened after cooking to prevent their skins from toughening.

Dried fruits such as prunes, apricots and peaches rehydrate and plump up beautifully in a very short time. Put the fruit in a container, pour over sufficient water, fruit juice or tea, cover and cook on HIGH (100%) for about 8 minutes. Allow a standing time of 10 minutes before using.

To plump up raisins, etc., for puddings and cakes, put them in a container with a little water, orange juice, tea, sherry or wine. Cook, covered, on HIGH (100%) for about 3 minutes. Stand for 5 minutes. Allow the fruit to cool before using it.

Meringue Toppings (see also pages 112 and 131)
Meringue toppings on fruit, for example, set well in the microwave but they will not brown and crisp. You may like to brown lightly the microwave-cooked meringue under a hot grill. Alternatively, a sprinkling of toasted coconut (page 107), demerara sugar or toasted nuts (page 129) looks attractive.

Milk Puddings (see also pages 120 and 121)
Your microwave can help you prepare creamy milk puddings such as rice, semolina or tapioca. A milk pudding should be prepared in a very large container – the milk will rise up dramatically. Put the rice, semolina or tapioca with the milk and sugar in a large, deep container and stir well. Cook on HIGH (100%) until boiling. Continue cooking on MEDIUM-LOW (30%), stirring occasionally, until thick and creamy.

Pancakes
These cannot be cooked by microwaves but they do reheat successfully. Prepare fillings such as fruit and nuts in the microwave and use these to fill pancakes which have been cooked in the frying pan. Simply reheat them on MEDIUM (50%) just before serving.

Pastry Dishes (see also page 133)
A shortcrust pastry case cooks well in the microwave, but it will not brown and crisp. When making flans, you may prefer to cook the flan case conventionally and the filling by microwave. Double crust pies are not successful – the bottom layer does not cook and the fruit filling boils out of the top. They reheat well though – but take care – the filling becomes very hot while the pastry remains only warm to the touch.

Suet crust pastry can be cooked in the microwave – cover it to keep it moist. Take care not to over-cook or the pastry will dry out and toughen. Follow the instructions on page 81.

Puff and flaky pastry do not cook well in the microwave. They need the dry heat of a conventional oven or a combination cooker to produce good results. With care, they reheat successfully in the microwave though.

Soufflés
Hot soufflés do not microwave successfully. They need the external heat of a conventional oven to crisp the surface and hold their shape.

Ingredients for cold soufflés can be prepared in the microwave – gelatine (page 107), orange and lemon juice (page 31), blanched and toasted nuts (page 129).

Sponge and Suet Puddings (see also pages 121 and 123)
These cook in a few minutes instead of hours of steaming on the hob. Cook on HIGH (100%). A sponge pudding takes about 3–6 minutes and a suet pudding about 5–6 minutes. The pudding should be removed from the

microwave when it is still slightly moist on top. It will continue cooking during a 5 minute standing time (over-cooking produces a dry texture).

Soften butter in the microwave before mixing sponge puddings or toppings. 100g/4 oz takes about 30 seconds on MEDIUM-LOW (30%).

Grease pudding basins in the usual way, for easy removal of the cooked pudding. Allow plenty of room for the pudding to rise during microwave cooking – the size increase is dramatic, though the pudding shrinks slightly when the microwave power is switched off.

When experimenting with your favourite recipes you will need to increase the quantity of liquid since it evaporates quickly: add about 15ml/1 tbsp extra per egg. Cover puddings loosely with non-stick or greased greaseproof paper to keep moisture in and to allow the puddings to rise.

Soften jams, syrup and honey to top your sponge mixtures. For easy measuring, soften golden syrup (in a jar, not in a tin!) on HIGH (100%) for 20–30 seconds. If a recipe requires clear honey and you have only the crystallised sort, heat it on HIGH (100%) to soften and clarify it before using.

RECIPES FOR DESSERTS AND PUDDINGS

Apples: Baked

Microwave-baked apples have a lovely flavour, though do not expect their skins to cook like those baked tradition-ally.
1. Core medium-sized cooking apples and slit the skin round the middle of each. Arrange in a circle on a plate.
2. Fill their centres with sugar and butter; a mixture of dried fruit, sugar and spices; or some marzipan.
3. Cook, uncovered, on HIGH (100%) for 6–8 minutes for

4 apples. They should be just cooked but still holding their shape.
4. Allow a standing time of 5 minutes before checking whether they are cooked. If necessary, microwave for an extra 1–2 minutes before standing them again for 5 minutes.

Hint: If you find that the apples burst out of their skins, try cooking on MEDIUM (50%) for 8–10 minutes.

Apple Meringue

Serves 4

700g (1½ lb) cooking apples, peeled, cored and sliced
50g (2 oz) granulated sugar
flavouring such as cloves, cinnamon, mixed spice, vanilla, grated orange or lemon rind, to taste
2 egg whites
100g (4 oz) caster sugar
flaked almonds, toasted

Method
1. Put the apples in a container with the granulated sugar and flavouring(s). Cook on HIGH (100%) for about 5 minutes until tender, stirring frequently.
2. Whisk the egg whites until they form stiff peaks, then whisk in half the caster sugar. Fold in the remaining caster sugar, then spread the meringue over the top of the apples.
3. Sprinkle with almonds and cook, uncovered, on MEDIUM (50%) for 3–4 minutes until set.
4. Brown lightly under a grill if wished.

Apple (or Fruit) Pie

Cook the apple (or fruit) filling in the microwave, then bake the pie in the conventional oven. 700g/1½ lb peeled, cored and sliced apples take about 5 minutes in a covered container on HIGH (100%), stirring occasionally.

Biscuit Crumb Base or Case

Use this as a base for a cheesecake or as a flan case for chilled cream dishes, or jellies.

75g (3 oz) butter
225g (8 oz) digestive or gingernut biscuits, crushed
50g (2 oz) sugar (optional)

Method
1. Heat the butter in a container on HIGH (100%) for 1–2 minutes or until melted.
2. Stir in the biscuit crumbs and sugar if used.
3. Base-line an 18cm/7 in flan dish with non-stick paper to ensure easy removal of the base or case.
4. To make a base only, press half the mixture over the dish. (Use the other half to make another base for freezing.) To make a case, press the mixture into the dish to cover the base and sides.
5. Cool in the refrigerator before filling.

Bread and Butter Pudding

Cooking times will vary with different microwaves but, once mastered, the result is excellent.

Serves 4

6 bread slices, lightly buttered
30–45ml (2–3 tbsp) raisins and/or sultanas
450ml (¾ pt) milk
2 eggs
40g (1½ oz) caster sugar

Method
1. Arrange the bread slices (cut them if necessary) in a straight-sided dish, sprinkling each layer with dried fruit.

2. Heat the milk on HIGH (100%) for 2–3 minutes until it is hot but not quite boiling.
3. Beat together the eggs and sugar and stir in the hot milk.
4. Strain the custard over the bread and allow to stand for 30 minutes.
5.. Put the dish in a larger container with sufficient hot water (from the kettle) to come half way up its sides.
6. Cook on MEDIUM (50%) for about 15 minutes or until just set.
7. Brown lightly under a hot grill if wished.

Bread Pudding

The appearance of this traditional spicy pudding is not so appetising when cooked in the microwave, though the flavour and texture are lovely. A topping of fruit such as sliced apples, brushed with golden syrup, added during the final half of cooking, improves appearance. Alternatively, brush the top with a jam glaze (page 118) when the pudding has cooled.

Serves 4

225g (8 oz) bread, cut into small pieces
300ml (½ pt) milk
1 egg, beaten
50g (2 oz) butter, melted
10ml (2 tsp) mixed spice
50g (2 oz) mixed peel
175g (6 oz) dried mixed fruit
demerara sugar

Method
1. Soak the bread for about 30 minutes, then mix in the egg, butter, spice, peel and fruit.
2. Pour the mixture into a lightly buttered, straight-sided

dish and cook, uncovered, on MEDIUM (50%) for 10 minutes, until just firm.
3. Allow the pudding to stand for 10 minutes.
4. Cook on MEDIUM (50%) for a further 10 minutes.
5. Sprinkle the top with demerara sugar and allow it to stand again before serving hot or cold.

Castle Puddings

Serves 6
1. Butter a six-mould muffin or bun tray and place a small spoonful of jam in each.
2. Top with Victoria Sandwich mixture (see page 131) flavoured with vanilla or almond essence.
3. Cook, covered loosely with non-stick or greased greaseproof paper (the puddings must have room to rise), on HIGH (100%) for 2–3 minutes until set but still slightly moist on the surface.
4. Allow a standing time of 5 minutes before turning out and serving with custard or cream.

Handy hint: Individual puddings can also be cooked in suitable buttered cups – one at a time. One pudding takes about 1 minute on HIGH (100%).

Chocolate Pudding

Conventional recipes, in which the chocolate, butter, sugar and liquid are heated together first, are suitable for microwave cooking. Cook on HIGH (100%) for 4–6 minutes.

Alternatively, use the recipe for Victoria Sandwich on page 131, replacing 15ml/1 tbsp flour with cocoa powder. Cover loosely with non-stick or greased greaseproof paper and cook on HIGH (100%) for 5–6 minutes, until set but still slightly moist on the surface. Stand for 5 minutes before serving.

Condé: Fruit

Serves 4–6
1. Prepare a rice pudding using the recipe on page 120.
2. Allow to cool before stirring in some double cream and chopped fresh or tinned fruit.
3. Chill before serving.

Custard Tart

Serves 4

18cm (7 in) shortcrust pastry case
2 eggs (size 2)
40g (1½ oz) caster sugar
500ml (¾ pt) milk
grated nutmeg

Method
1. *Either* cook the pastry in the microwave following the directions on page 133.
   Or bake the pastry in the conventional oven.
2. Beat the eggs with the sugar. Stir in the milk.
3. Strain the custard into the pastry case (which should be in a microwave-safe container). Grate some nutmeg over the top.
4. Cook on MEDIUM-LOW (30%) until the custard is just set.
5. Allow a standing time of 5 minutes.

Handy hint: Heat the custard on MEDIUM (50%), stirring frequently, until it begins to set before pouring it into the pastry case. Finish cooking as above – the cooking time will be shorter.

Egg Custard, Baked

The microwave produces superb baked egg custard once

you have mastered the technique and timing to suit your particular microwave. Check with your instruction book to see which setting it recommends for this dish. Alternatively, try the method below.

Serves 4

600ml (1 pt) milk
vanilla essence
4 eggs (size 2)
40g (1½ oz) caster sugar
grated nutmeg

Method
1. Put the milk in a jug with a few drops of vanilla essence. Cook on HIGH (100%) for 2–3 minutes until hot but not boiling.
2. Beat the eggs with the sugar. Whisk in the hot milk, then strain the mixture into a 900ml/1½ pt dish. Sprinkle some grated nutmeg over the top.
3. Place the dish in a large container and pour round sufficient hot water (from the kettle) to come half way up its sides.
4. Cook on MEDIUM (50%) for 15–20 minutes until just set.
5. Allow a standing time of 5–10 minutes before serving hot, warm or chilled.

Fruit Flan

Prepare a shortcrust pastry case. Microwave cooking instructions appear on page 133, or it may be cooked conventionally for a crisp finish.

Fill the case with fresh fruit, fruit cooked in the microwave (see page 108), or drained tinned fruit.

Coat with a jam glaze (page 118) or fruit juice thickened with gelatine (page 107). Alternatively, use arrowroot: blend 5–10ml/1–2 tsp arrowroot with some fruit juice in a small container. Cook, uncovered, on HIGH (100%) stirring frequently until the mixture thickens. Pour or brush this over the fruit.

Jam Glaze

Use this for topping fruit, sponge puddings or fruit flans, and for glazing cakes to give an attractive finish. Make sure the container is suitable for high-temperature cooking.

1. Put about 100g/4 oz jam, such as apricot, in a bowl with 10ml/2 tsp lemon juice and 15ml/1 tbsp water.
2. Cook, uncovered, on HIGH (100%) for 1–2 minutes, until melted, stirring occasionally.
3. Sieve if necessary and serve hot or chilled.

Lemon Curd

Makes about 900g/2 lb – use within 2 weeks

grated rind and juice of 4 lemons
100g (4 oz) unsalted butter
450g (1 lb) caster sugar
4 eggs (size 2), beaten

Method
1. Put the lemon rind and juice, butter and sugar in a large container and cook on HIGH (100%) for 4 minutes, until the butter melts.
2. Stir the mixture well to dissolve the sugar and to mix in the melted butter.
3. Add the beaten eggs and stir well.
4. Cook, uncovered, on HIGH (100%) for 5–6 minutes, stirring every minute until the mixture is thick and creamy.
5. Cool slightly before potting and refrigerating.

Lemon Meringue Pie

Serves 6

30ml (2 tbsp) cornflour
125g (5 oz) caster sugar
grated rind and juice of 2 large lemons
150ml (¼ pt) water
2 eggs, separated
15g (½ oz) butter, cubed
20.5cm (8 in) shortcrust pastry case, cooked

Method
1. Put the cornflour, 50g/2 oz sugar and lemon rind into a bowl and mix to a smooth paste with the water and lemon juice.
2. Cook on HIGH (100%) for 2–3 minutes until boiling and thickened, stirring frequently.
3. Beat in the egg yolks and butter. Cook on HIGH (100%) for 30 seconds, then pour into the flan case.
4. Beat the egg whites until stiff and gently fold in the remaining sugar. Pile the meringue on top of the flan.
5. Cook on MEDIUM (50%) for 3–4 minutes until set. Brown lightly under a grill if wished.

Macaroni Pudding

Serves 4

175g (6 oz) macaroni
600ml (1 pt) milk
40g (1½ oz) sugar

Method
1. Put the macaroni, milk and sugar in a large, deep container.
2. Cover and cook on HIGH (100%) for 10–15 minutes, stirring occasionally.

3. Allow the pudding to stand, covered, for 10 minutes. Stir well before serving.

Queen of Puddings

Serves 4

450ml (¾ pt) milk
25g (1 oz) butter
2 eggs, separated
50g (2 oz) caster sugar
grated rind of ½ lemon
75g (3 oz) fresh breadcrumbs
30ml (2 tbsp) jam

Method
1. Put the milk, butter, egg yolks, 25g/1 oz sugar and the lemon rind in a jug.
2. Cook on HIGH (100%) for 2½–3 minutes, stirring twice.
3. Stir in the breadcrumbs and pour into a dish.
4. Melt the jam on HIGH (100%) for 30 seconds and trickle it over the breadcrumb mixture.
5. Whisk the egg whites until they form stiff peaks. Fold in the remaining sugar, then spoon the meringue on top.
6. Cook, uncovered, on MEDIUM (50%) for 3–4 minutes until set. Brown lightly under a grill if wished.

Rice Pudding

Rice pudding cooked in the microwave is deliciously creamy.

Serves 4

600ml (1 pt) milk
50g (2 oz) pudding rice
40g (1½ oz) sugar
butter
grated nutmeg

Method
1. Put the milk, rice and sugar in a large, deep container.
2. Dot the pudding with butter and sprinkle with grated nutmeg.
3. Cook on HIGH (100%) for about 5 minutes until boiling. Stir well.
4. Cover and cook on MEDIUM-LOW (30%) for about 30 minutes or more until thickened, stirring every 10 minutes.
5. Allow a standing time of 5 minutes before serving.

Handy hint: The longer the pudding cooks, the more creamy it becomes. If you prefer a pudding with a skin on top, transfer it to a suitable container and brown the top lightly under a grill before serving.

Semolina Pudding

Serves 4

600ml (1 pt) milk
60ml (4 tbsp) semolina
caster sugar

Method
1. Blend the milk, semolina and sugar to taste in a large, deep container.
2. Cook on HIGH (100%) for about 5 minutes or until boiling, stirring occasionally.
3. Stir well, cover and cook on MEDIUM-LOW (30%) for about 10 minutes, stirring frequently.
4. Allow the pudding to stand for 5 minutes before serving.

Sponge Pudding: Jam

Serves 4

1. Place 30–45ml/2–3 tbsp jam into a buttered 1.1 litre/ 2 pt basin. Top with a quantity of Victoria Sandwich mix (page 131).

2. Cover loosely with non-stick or greased greaseproof paper (the pudding must have space to rise) and cook on HIGH (100%) for 5–6 minutes. It should look slightly moist on the surface.
3. Stand the pudding for 5 minutes before turning it out.

Spotted Dick

This pudding is cooked in a microwave or roasting bag.

Serves 4

50g (2 oz) mixed dried fruit
50g (2 oz) shredded suet
25g (1 oz) sugar
pinch of salt
100g (4 oz) self-raising flour, sifted
milk

Method
1. Mix the dried fruit, suet, sugar, salt and flour.
2. Stir in sufficient milk to make a soft dough.
3. Put the mixture in a roasting bag or microwave bag. Tie the opening loosely (use a piece of string or a strip of the bag, cut off from the end), allowing room for the pudding to expand and for steam to escape.
4. Place the bag in a large container with 600ml/1 pt boiling water (from the kettle) – tied end upwards, out of the water.
5. Cook on HIGH (100%) for 12–15 minutes, turning the pudding half way through cooking.
6. Allow the pudding to stand for 5 minutes before draining and serving with custard.

Strawberry Shortcake

Shortbread cooks well in the microwave and is ideal for

decorating with fruit and cream. The recipe appears on page 136. When the shortbread is cool, decorate it with whipped cream and fresh strawberries, raspberries, blackberries or peaches.

Suet Pudding with Jam

Serves 4

30ml (2 tbsp) jam
100g (4 oz) self-raising flour
pinch of salt
50g (2 oz) caster sugar
50g (2 oz) shredded suet
1 egg, beaten
milk

Method
1. Put the jam into the base of a buttered 900ml/1½ pt pudding basin.
2. Sieve the flour and salt. Stir in the sugar, suet, egg and sufficient milk to form a soft mixture.
3. Top the jam with the suet mixture and cover loosely with non-stick or greased greaseproof paper.
4. Cook on MEDIUM (50%) for 7–10 minutes or until the surface of the pudding springs back into shape when pressed gently with your fingers.
5. Allow a standing time of 5 minutes before turning out.

Ring the changes: Replace the jam with marmalade, honey, syrup, stewed fruit such as apples or rhubarb, canned fruit or pie fillings.

Summer Pudding

Prepare the fruits for this in the microwave. Follow the hints on page 108.

Serves 4–6

1. Line a buttered 900ml/1½ pt pudding basin with bread slices (trimmed of their crusts).
2. Cook soft fruits such as raspberries and redcurrants with sugar to taste. (See page 108.)
3. Drain off some of the cooking liquid and reserve this for serving with the pudding.
4. Fill the pudding with fruit and cover with more bread, right to the edges.
5. Put a plate on top of the pudding with a weight on top of that. Chill overnight before turning out or serving from the basin with the reserved juice.

Treacle Tart

This works best when the flan case is made with a rich shortcrust pastry and this must be cooked in the conventional oven. Alternatively, buy a pre-cooked sweet pastry case.

Serves 4–6

90ml (6 tbsp) golden syrup
50g (2 oz) fresh breadcrumbs
lemon juice and grated lemon rind
20.5cm (8 in) flan case, cooked

Method
1. Mix together the golden syrup and breadcrumbs and stir in a little lemon juice and rind.
2. Spread the mixture over the base of the flan case.
3. Cook on HIGH (100%) for 3–5 minutes.
4. Allow a standing time of 5 minutes before serving hot or cold.

Upside-down Pudding

Serves 4–6

125g (5 oz) butter
25g (1 oz) brown sugar
411g can of fruit (pineapple, apricot halves, peach slices,
  pear halves, cherries), drained
75g (3 oz) caster sugar
2 eggs, beaten
100g (4 oz) self-raising flour
milk

Method
1. Melt 25g/1 oz butter in a straight-sided 20.5cm/8 in dish on HIGH (100%) for about 30 seconds. Tilt the dish to spread the butter over its base.
2. Sprinkle the brown sugar over the butter and arrange the fruit in this.
3. Beat together the remaining butter and the caster sugar until light and fluffy. Gradually add the eggs, beating well, then fold in the flour. Add sufficient milk to form a soft dropping consistency. Spread the mixture evenly over the fruit.
4. Cook, uncovered, on HIGH (100%) for 6–9 minutes.
5. Allow a standing time of 10 minutes before turning out of the container.

10
CAKES, PASTRY AND BISCUITS

HANDY HINTS FOR CAKE-MAKING

Microwaved cakes rise well and their flavour is good. The texture will be slightly different from cakes cooked in a conventional oven and, of course, they will not brown or crisp. Once you have accepted this difference I am sure you will want to try your own recipes in the microwave.

Recipes which involve melting together ingredients such as fat, sugar and syrup are particularly suitable for microwave cooking.

Fat-free sponges of the whisked type are best cooked

conventionally. If you do cook them in the microwave, take care as they easily over-cook.

Rich fruit cakes (including Christmas cake) can be cooked in the microwave. Cook them on MEDIUM-LOW (30%). A 20.5cm/8 in straight-sided, round cake takes 45 minutes – 1 hour. When cooked, the top of the cake should appear slightly uncooked but a skewer inserted in the centre should come out clean.

The shape of a cake container is important (see page 13). A ring shape is the most succesful for any cake. Round containers are the next best choice. Squares and oblongs are generally not suitable because the corners tend to over-cook and dry out.

Line containers with non-stick paper or greased grease-proof paper to assist with easy removal of cakes. Never flour the container or an unpalatable crust will form on the outside of the cake.

Half-fill the cooking container only, to allow the cake to rise. It will shrink a little on removal from the oven.

Dried fruit can be plumped up in the microwave before adding it to a cake mixture. This helps to produce cakes which are beautifully moist. In a bowl, cover 225g/8 oz raisins, currants or sultanas with 150ml (¼ pt) water, fruit juice or cold tea. Cook, covered, on HIGH (100%) for 3 minutes. Allow to stand for 5 minutes. Cool and use.

Cakes can dry out quickly in the microwave so add extra liquid when adapting your favourite recipes – about 15ml/ 1 tbsp per egg for light cakes; fruit cake mixtures should have a very soft dropping consistency.

Make sure that sugar is well blended into the mix – lumps of sugar burn easily in the microwave.

To decide which power level to use – check with a similar recipe in your instruction book. Generally, plain cakes are cooked on HIGH (100%) (though you may find better results are achieved on lower powers), while fruit cakes are cooked on MEDIUM-LOW (30%).

Cook one cake at a time. Cakes over 20.5cm/8 in diameter are not generally successful. Stand all cakes on a rack to encourage even cooking. To help a cake rise evenly, you may find that you need to turn it occasionally if your microwave does not have an automatic turntable.

Cooking times will depend on the type and size of cake. The cake should be removed from the microwave when it still looks slightly moist on its surface.

Small cakes should be arranged in a circle. If you put one in the middle it will cook much more slowly than the others.

Allow a standing time of 5–10 minutes before turning the cake out of its container. Allow 20 minutes for a fruit cake – any wet areas on the side of the turned-out cake will dry out as it stands.

Extra colouring can be added in the form of brown sugar, wholemeal flour, cocoa, chocolate, and so on. Sprinkle pale-looking cakes with a coating of icing sugar or add a tempting topping of icing, marzipan, a jam glaze on fruit and nuts, or toasted coconut or nuts.

Thaw cakes in the microwave. Place on a sheet of absorbent paper and cook on DEFROST (30%):

> 1 small (fairy) cake or individual slice of cake takes 15–30 seconds
> 2 small (fairy) cakes take about 30 seconds
> 4 small (fairy) cakes take 1–2 minutes.
> A 20.5cm/8 in cake takes 2–3 minutes.

Allow a defrosting-standing time of 2 minutes for small cakes and 5–10 minutes for large cakes.

Take care when thawing cakes with a cream filling or decoration. The cream may melt before the cake defrosts. It is better to allow these to thaw naturally.

Additional tips

Soften sugar by placing it in a dish with a slice of lemon and heating on HIGH (100%) for 30 seconds – 1 minute.

Measure golden syrup easily – see page 111.

Clarify honey – see page 111.

Melt chocolate – see page 107.

Toast coconut – see page 107.

Blanch almonds. Bring about 300ml/½ pt water to the boil on HIGH (100%). Add some almonds and cook on HIGH (100%) for 2 minutes. Drain the almonds and when they are cool enough to handle, rub off their skins.

Toast nuts, including almonds, by one of these methods.
1. Spread blanched, skinned nuts (halved or chopped) on a plate and cook, uncovered, on HIGH (100%) until they turn golden brown. Stir the nuts frequently during cooking.
2. Place a small quantity of skinned, halved or chopped nuts in a small container with a small knob of butter. Cook, uncovered, on HIGH (100%) until they turn golden brown. Stir or shake the nuts frequently to encourage even browning. Take care when handling the dish – it becomes very hot.

Dry breadcrumbs
Cut four slices of bread into small cubes and arrange them on an ovenproof plate. Cook on HIGH (100%) for about 4 minutes, checking and shaking them every minute, or until they are dry enough to crumble.

Toasted (buttered) breadcrumbs
175g/6 oz breadcrumbs need about 50g/2 oz butter. Melt the butter on HIGH (100%) for about 1 minute. Stir in the breadcrumbs and coat them well with the butter. Cook, uncovered, on HIGH (100%) for about 10 minutes or until golden brown, stirring frequently.

CAKE RECIPES

Date and Carrot Cake

Sandwich the two layers with cream cheese sweetened with vanilla-flavoured sugar. See the note on page 111 for measuring golden syrup.

175g (6 oz) butter
175g (6 oz) light brown sugar
90ml (6 tbsp) golden syrup
275g (10 oz) self-raising flour
10ml (2 tsp) mixed spice
pinch of salt
3 eggs, beaten
225g (8 oz) carrots, finely grated
175g (6 oz) stoned dates, chopped

Method
1. Put the butter, sugar and syrup in a large container and cook on HIGH (100%) for 2–3 minutes.
2. Stir in the flour, mixed spice and salt.
3. Beat in the eggs, then add the carrots and dates.

4. Divide the mixture between two greased 18cm/7 in containers. Lining the base with non-stick paper helps the cakes turn out easily.
5. Cook *each* container (one at a time), uncovered, for 6–8 minutes on HIGH (100%) until set but still slightly moist on top.
6. Cool slightly before turning the cakes out of their containers on to a cooling rack lined with non-stick paper. Cool completely.

Meringues

Meringue mixture for cooking in the microwave needs to be very stiff if it is to hold its shape. Use 275–350g/10–12 oz icing sugar to one egg white (size 3). This sounds like a great deal of sugar, but it does make about 20 small meringues which can be sandwiched together with whipped cream. Beat together the egg white and icing sugar to make a firm paste. Divide into small balls. Arrange eight at a time in a circle on a plate or turntable covered with non-stick paper. Cook, uncovered, on HIGH (100%) for 1½–2 minutes until risen and firm to the touch. They are cooked when they do not shrink on opening the oven door. Allow to cool before carefully peeling off the paper.

Victoria Sandwich

175g (6 oz) self-raising flour
175g (6 oz) soft butter or margarine
175g (6 oz) caster sugar
3 eggs
45ml (3 tbsp) milk
few drops vanilla essence
jam
icing sugar

Method

1. Lightly butter a 20.5cm/8 in soufflé dish and line its base with a circle of microwave or non-stick paper.
2. Sift the flour into a large bowl and add the butter, sugar, eggs, milk and vanilla essence. Beat until smooth. Spoon the mixture into the prepared dish, levelling the surface and making a slight well in the centre.
3. Stand the dish on a microwave or roasting rack and cook, uncovered, on HIGH (100%) for 6–7 minutes until risen. The surface of the cake should still look slightly moist at the centre top, but the cake beneath it should be cooked.
4. Leave to stand in its dish for 5 minutes (the surface will finish drying) before turning out on to a wire rack lined with non-stick paper. Leave to cool completely.
5. Split the cake and fill with jam. Sift icing sugar over the top before serving.

Ring the changes: Make a *chocolate cake* by replacing 30ml/2 tbsp flour with the same quantity of cocoa. Alternatively, flavour the cake with orange or lemon rind and juice.

HANDY HINTS FOR COOKING PASTRY

A shortcrust pastry case cooks well in the microwave – it is crisp and has a good flavour. It is best cooked without a filling – this can be added to the flan case later. Double crust pies are disastrous in the microwave since the base will not cook and the filling will overflow. Pastry containing sugar is not successful since the sugar tends to burn. Puff pastry is best cooked conventionally. Suet pastry cooks well so long as it is covered to retain maximum moisture.

Thawing pastry dishes is successful though an empty pastry flan case can be filled (and cooked) from frozen. Large flans, quiches and tarts from the freezer should be microwaved on DEFROST (30%) for about 4 minutes, then allowed to stand for 5 minutes. If it is still icy, return it to the microwave for a further 1–2 minutes on DEFROST (30%) before standing it again.

Large pies are difficult to defrost since the pastry defrosts before the filling and is liable to heat up while the filling is still frozen. Microwave on DEFROST (30%) until the pastry is just warm to touch, then allow the pie to thaw naturally in a cool place.

Reheating pastry dishes

Many pastry dishes which cannot be cooked successfully by microwaves will, in fact, reheat in the microwave with good results. Beware of over-heating though or the pastry will become soggy. Individual portions of flans, pies, etc., need only ½–1 minute on HIGH (100%). Microwave them in the serving dish or on a sheet of absorbent paper.

Sausage rolls: Four take about 1 minute on HIGH (100%). One sausage roll takes about 15 seconds.

Cooked, filled *vol-au-vents* reheat well. Make their filling in the microwave too – see page 102 for hints on sauce-making.

PASTRY RECIPES

Shortcrust Pastry Case

Rolling the pastry out using wholemeal flour helps give an attractive colour to otherwise pale pastry. Do not add sugar to the pastry – it will burn. Use milk instead of water to mix the dough – this gives a better result.
1. Line a suitable flan dish with the pastry, prick the pastry case all over with a fork, particularly at the bend in the dish.
2. Cover the pastry base with two layers of absorbent kitchen paper to absorb the steam. Place an upturned plate or saucer on the paper.

3. Cook on HIGH (100%) (about 6 minutes for a 20.5cm/8 in flan) until the pastry is firm to the touch and is beginning to shrink away from the sides of the dish.
4. Stand for 5 minutes. Remove the plate and paper.

Bakewell Tart

1. Prepare and cook a shortcrust pastry case following the hints above. Allow it to cool. Alternatively, buy a pre-baked sweet pastry case.
2. Spread a layer of jam over the base of the flan case and top with a Victoria Sandwich mix flavoured with almond essence (recipe page 131).
3. Cook, uncovered, on MEDIUM (50%) for 7–10 minutes until the cake is just firm to touch.
4. *Either* allow it to stand for 5 minutes before serving hot. *Or* cool the tart and top with thin icing and toasted flaked almonds.

Quiche or Savoury Flan: See recipe on page 60.

Scones

Scones are best cooked conventionally. If you do cook them in the microwave, use a browning dish and follow a recipe in the manufacturer's instruction book.

HINTS FOR COOKING BISCUITS
Cookie-type biscuits are the most suitable for cooking in the microwave – six biscuits at a time on a sheet of non-stick or greaseproof paper. Best results are obtained when cooked on MEDIUM (50%). Six take about 2–3 minutes. Stand for 5 minutes before lifting off the paper and cooling on a wire rack. Cooking on HIGH (100%) tends to produce rather dry, harder biscuits. Of course you will not achieve traditional golden colours, but biscuits can be

sprinkled with chopped nuts or cherries before cooking or with icing sugar after cooking, or you could decorate them with chocolate (half-dipping gives attractive results) or icing.

BISCUIT RECIPES

Flapjacks

These will not be quite so crisp when cooked by microwave. See page 111 for an easy way to measure golden syrup.

Makes 8 pieces

45ml (3 tbsp) golden syrup
100g (4 oz) sugar
100g (4 oz) butter
225g (8 oz) rolled oats
1 egg, beaten
5ml (1 tsp) baking powder
pinch of salt

Method
1. Put the golden syrup, sugar and butter in a container. Cook on HIGH (100%) for 2–3 minutes or until the sugar has dissolved.
2. Stir in the rolled oats with the beaten egg, baking powder and salt.
3. Spread the mixture into a round, shallow container (18–20.5cm/7–8 in) lined with non-stick or greased greaseproof paper.
4. Cook on HIGH (100%) for 4–6 minutes, turning the dish once or twice in microwaves without turntables.
5. Allow to stand for 5 minutes, then mark into sections with a knife.
6. Allow the flapjacks to cool in the container before cutting them.

Shortbread

Makes 6–8 pieces

110g (4 oz) butter
50g (2 oz) caster sugar
150g (5 oz) plain flour
25g (1 oz) fine semolina

Method
1. Cream together the butter and sugar until they are light and fluffy.
2. Sieve the flour and semolina and fold these gently into the mixture. Knead the mixture lightly to form a dough.
3. Roll out or press the dough into a round greased and base-lined 18cm/7 in flan dish or on to a plate lined with greased greaseproof paper.
4. Prick the dough well with a fork and cook, uncovered, on HIGH (100%) for about 4 minutes or until set.
5. Allow to stand for 5 minutes, then cut into triangles, and sprinkle with caster sugar.
6. When cool, break the shortbread into portions.

11
PRESERVES AND SWEETS

HINTS FOR MAKING PRESERVES
Jams, marmalades and chutneys can be made in the microwave, and both colour and flavour are good. They do not burn on the cooking container and generally need far less attention than preserves prepared conventionally on the hob. Small quantities are particularly suitable for cooking in the microwave.

Use a very large container. The preserve must have plenty of room to boil up. Always use a container which is suitable for high temperature cooking – sugar mixtures become very hot. The container will get hot too, so use oven gloves.

Do not try to cook more than 1.5kg/3 lb fruit – larger quantities are best cooked on the hob.

Most soft fruits need no additional liquid. Fruits with skins (plums and gooseberries) need about 15ml/1 tbsp water per 450g/1 lb.

Cook on HIGH (100%) unless you think the preserve may bubble over, in which case reduce the power level to MEDIUM (50%) and cook for longer.

Check for setting point by dropping a small amount of preserve on to a chilled saucer – if a skin forms, the jam, jelly or marmalade is ready to set.

If you use a sugar thermometer, never leave it in the microwave cooker when it is switched on – unless it is specifically designed for use in the microwave. Setting point is 104–105°C/220–222°F.

To Sterilise Jars:
Quarter-fill up to four jars with water and arrange them in a circle in the microwave. Cook on HIGH (100%) until the water boils. Using oven gloves, carefully lift the jars out of the microwave and empty out the water. Invert the jars on to a clean tea towel or kitchen paper. Use as required.

RECIPES FOR PRESERVES

Raspberry Jam

Makes about 700g/1½ lb

450g (1 lb) raspberries, washed and drained
15ml (1 tbsp) water
450g (1 lb) caster sugar

Method
1. Put the raspberries and water into a large, heatproof bowl.
2. Cook on HIGH (100%) for about 4 minutes, stirring once or twice, until the fruit is soft.
3. Stir in the sugar and cook on HIGH (100%) for 2 minutes, stirring frequently, until the sugar dissolves.
4. Continue cooking, uncovered, on HIGH (100%) for about 10–12 minutes, stirring every minute or so, until setting point is reached.
5. Cool, pot and label the jam.

Redcurrant Jelly

900g (2 lb) redcurrants, washed and drained
200ml (7 fl oz) water
450g (1 lb) caster sugar to each 600ml/1 pt juice

Method
1. Put the redcurrants and the water in a large, deep container.
2. Cook on HIGH (100%), stirring occasionally, until the fruit boils and turns to a rough purée.
3. Allow the mixture to cool before tipping it into a fine nylon sieve, muslin or a jelly bag. Allow the juice to strain through. This may take several hours but do not press the fruit through or the jelly will be cloudy.
4. Measure the liquid and add 450g/1 lb sugar to each 600ml/1 pt juice. Tip into a large heatproof bowl.
5. Cook on HIGH (100%), stirring occasionally, until the sugar dissolves.
6. Continue to cook, uncovered, on HIGH (100%) until setting point is reached.
7. Cool, pot and label the jelly.

Apple Jelly

900g (2 lb) cooking or crab apples, diced with the peel and core left on
450ml (¾ pt) water
450g (1 lb) caster sugar to each 600ml/1 pt juice

Method
Follow steps 1–7 as for Redcurrant Jelly.

Mint Jelly

Makes about 900g/2 lb

40g (1½ oz) fresh mint leaves
450g (1 lb) caster sugar
300ml (½ pt) vinegar
225ml (8 fl oz) certo (bottled pectin)
green food colouring
15g (½ oz) chopped mint

Method
1. Mix together the mint leaves, sugar and vinegar in a large, heatproof bowl.
2. Cook on HIGH (100%) for 8–10 minutes or until the sugar dissolves, stirring occasionally.
3. Bring to the boil on HIGH (100%) and cook for a further 1 minute.
4. Strain the mixture through a fine nylon sieve, muslin or a jelly bag (do not be tempted to squeeze the mint leaves).
5. Stir in the bottled pectin and a little green food colouring.
6. Cook, uncovered, on HIGH (100%) for 4–5 minutes, stirring once or twice, then stir in the chopped mint.
7. Cool, pot and label the jelly.

Marmalade

Makes about 1kg/2½ lb

2 lemons
1kg (2 lb) Seville oranges
1kg (2 lb) sugar
knob of butter

Method
1. Warm the lemons on HIGH (100%) for 1 minute. Squeeze their juice into a large container.
2. Cut the rind from the oranges, avoiding the white pith. Cut the rind into shreds and set aside.
3. Put the orange flesh and pips into a food processor and chop. Add the mixture to the lemon juice with 900ml/ 1½ pt *boiling* water. Cover and cook on HIGH (100%) for about 15 minutes, stirring once or twice.
4. Tip the mixture into a sieve over a large heatproof bowl, pressing it until all the juice is extracted. Stir the orange shreds into the juice. Cover and cook on HIGH (100%) for about 15 minutes, stirring occasionally, until the rind is tender.
5. Add the sugar, stirring to dissolve it completely. Cook, uncovered, for about 10 minutes, stirring once, until setting point is reached.
6. Stir in the butter then, using a slotted spoon, remove any scum.
7. Leave to cool for 15 minutes, then pot, cover and label.

Apple Butter

Makes about 2kg/4 lb

up to 1kg (2 lb) cooking apples or sharp eating apples
sugar
butter
5ml (1 tsp) ground cinnamon

Method
1. Roughly chop the apples (don't peel or core them).
2. Put the apples into a large heatproof bowl. Cover and cook on HIGH (100%), stirring occasionally, until just soft (the cooking time will depend on the apples used).
3. Tip the mixture into a nylon sieve and press to extract the apple purée. Weigh the purée.
4. Weigh out 350g/12 oz sugar and 25g/1 oz butter for each 450g/1 lb apple purée.
5. Put the sugar into a bowl and warm on HIGH (100%) for 3–4 minutes.
6. Put the apple purée into a large heatproof bowl and stir in the warm sugar, butter and cinnamon.
7. Cook, uncovered, on HIGH (100%) until setting point is reached.
8. Allow to cool slightly then pot, cover and label.

Lemon Curd: See page 118.

Beetroot and Apple Chutney

Makes about 1.5kg/3 lb

450g (1 lb) beetroot
60ml (4 tbsp) water
450g (1 lb) cooking apples, peeled, cored and diced
225g (8 oz) onions, finely chopped
450ml (¾ pt) vinegar
2.5ml (½ tsp) ground cumin
2.5ml (½ tsp) celery salt
2.5ml (½ tsp) salt

Method
1. Put the washed (unpeeled) beetroot into a large container with the water. Cover and cook on HIGH (100%) for 7–8 minutes or until the beetroot is tender. Drain, cool, remove the skin and chop the beetroot finely.
2. Place the apples, onion, vinegar, spices and salt into a large heatproof bowl. Cover and cook on HIGH (100%) for about 5 minutes until the onion is soft.
3. Stir in the beetroot, cover and cook on HIGH (100%) for about 10 minutes. Uncover and cook on HIGH (100%) until the mixture has thickened. Stir once or twice during cooking.
4. Cool, pot and label the chutney.

Tomato Chutney

Makes about 900g/2 lb

700g (1½ lb) firm tomatoes
225g (8 oz) cooking apples, peeled, cored and chopped
1 medium onion, finely chopped
100g (4 oz) soft brown sugar
100g (4 oz) sultanas
5ml (1 tsp) salt
200ml (7 fl oz) malt vinegar
15g (½ oz) ground ginger
2.5ml (½ tsp) mustard powder
1.25ml (¼ tsp) cayenne pepper

Method
1. Put the tomatoes into a large heatproof bowl and pour over sufficient *boiling* water to just cover them. Cook for about 4 minutes then, one at a time, lift the tomatoes out of the water and remove and discard their skins. Roughly chop the skinned tomatoes.
2. Put the tomatoes into a large heatproof bowl and mix in the remaining ingredients. Cook, uncovered, on HIGH (100%) for about 30 minutes, stirring occasionally (and frequently once the mixture starts to thicken) until the chutney is thick and there is no pool of liquid.
3. Leave to cool slightly then pot, cover and label the chutney.

HINTS FOR MAKING SWEETS

Small quantities of sweets, toffee and fudge are easy to make with the microwave. They do not stick or burn and the results are good.

Use the microwave to melt chocolate to coat nuts and fruits and to make truffles.

Generally use a little less liquid since there is less evaporation in the microwave.

Use a container which is at least 3 times the size of the amount of sweet mixture. It may boil up dramatically. Sugar mixtures reach very high temperatures so make sure that you choose a container which is heatproof.

Use oven gloves – the container can get very hot.

Use a sugar thermometer, but never leave it in the mixture while the microwave energy is switched on unless it is a special microwave thermometer.

Check the temperature frequently to avoid over-cooking.

Do not cover the container when making sweets.

RECIPES FOR SWEETS

Chocolate Truffles

Makes 36

100g (4 oz) plain chocolate pieces
50g (2 oz) butter
15ml (1 tbsp) rum
25g (1 oz) ground almonds
25g (1 oz) fresh cake crumbs
225g (8 oz) icing sugar, sifted
drinking chocolate powder

Method
1. Melt the chocolate and butter on MEDIUM (50%) for 2–3 minutes, stirring occasionally, until melted.

2. Add the rum and mix in the remaining ingredients (except the drinking chocolate powder).
3. Chill until firm.
4. Shape into 36 balls and toss in some drinking chocolate powder.

Fudge

Makes about 225g/8 oz
See page 111 for easy measuring of golden syrup.

225g (8 oz) caster sugar
30ml (2 tbsp) golden syrup
25g (1 oz) butter
30ml (2 tbsp) orange juice
60ml (4 tbsp) condensed milk

Method
1. Put all the ingredients into a large, deep heatproof container.
2. Cook, uncovered, on HIGH (100%) for about 5 minutes, or until it reaches setting point. Drop a little into cold water – it should set. If using a sugar thermometer, the mixture should reach 115°C/238°F.
3. Beat the mixture, then pour it into a small lightly greased square tin.
4. Cut into squares when cold.

Toffee

Makes about 225g/8 oz
See page 111 for easy measuring of golden syrup.

110g (4 oz) golden syrup
110g (4 oz) granulated sugar
50g (2 oz) butter

Method
1. Place all the ingredients in a large, deep heatproof container.
2. Cook on HIGH (100%) for about 5 minutes, stirring occasionally, or until a little dropped in a cup of cold water sets. If using a sugar thermometer, it should reach 138°C/280°F.
3. Pour the toffee into a small lightly greased, square tin.
4. Cut into squares just before it is completely set.

Chocolate Crispies

Makes 12

225g (8 oz) plain chocolate
50g (2 oz) butter
15ml (1 tbsp) golden syrup
50g (2 oz) rice crispies or cornflakes

Method
1. Break the chocolate into a bowl and add the butter and syrup. Cook, uncovered, on MEDIUM (50%) for 4–5 minutes, stirring frequently until melted and smooth.
2. Gently stir in the rice crispies or cornflakes.
3. Spoon the mixture into 12 paper cake cases and leave to set.

Chocolate Fruit Clusters

Makes 12

40g (1½ oz) flaked almonds
75g (3 oz) plain or milk chocolate
25g (1 oz) raisins
25g (1 oz) no-soak dried apricots, finely chopped

Method
1. Put the almonds in a shallow ovenproof dish and cook, uncovered, on HIGH (100%) for 3–4 minutes until lightly browned, stirring frequently.
2. Break the chocolate into a bowl and cook on DEFROST (30%) for about 4 minutes, stirring occasionally, until melted. Stir in the almonds, raisins and apricots.
3. Spoon the mixture into 12 paper sweet cases and leave to set. Chill until firm.

INDEX

Words in italics refer to actual recipes.

Other Microwave Books By Annette Yates

MICROWAVE COOKING PROPERLY EXPLAINED

Annette Yates explains simply and clearly how a microwave oven works, and helps you choose the best equipment. Planned from first principles for both the present and prospective microwave owner, the book shows how the versatile microwave oven can transform life for the busy cook. Contains over 90 recipes.

MICROWAVE COOKING TIMES AT A GLANCE!

The essential guide for everyone with a microwave. Full of tips and hints about preparing and cooking different types of food, as well as the length of cooking time required, with tables giving at-a-glance advice for all wattages 500W to 1000W. Arranged in A-Z sequence for speedy reference.

THE COMBINATION MICROWAVE COOK

At last a cookbook written specifically for combination microwave cookers and for microwaves with built-in grills. Contains over 100 recipes.

MICROWAVE RECIPES FOR ONE

This book is designed specifically for the person who lives alone or who has to prepare individual meals for some other reason. It includes recipes for: breakfasts; soups; starters and sauces; fish, meat, poultry, vegetable, cheese, egg and pasta dishes; and desserts – PLUS an indispensable cooking guide which explains how to adapt family recipe instructions to the smaller amounts needed for a single portion.

THE STIR FRY COOK

If you're looking for quick, simple meals needing the minimum of preparation, equipment and washing-up, then search no further! Cook any of the 101 recipes selected by Caroline Young and you'll see how easy it is to create, all in one pan, a delicious dish in less than 30 minutes. All you need is a good frypan or wok.

Each recipe serves two people, but if you're cooking for four, just double the amount of ingredients.

REAL SOUPS & SAUCES

Annette Yates presents a feast of real soups for every season and reason: light and chilled for a warm summer's day; smooth, puréed or creamed for that formal occasion; hearty and thick — a meal in itself — for a cold winter evening. Discover, too, an array of ideas for attractive, tasty garnishes.

The book also contains subtle, rich, savoury, sweet, traditional and quick-to-make sauces that will transform everyday meals and turn that special party dish into a true culinary delight!

THE CURRY SECRET
This is the curry book with a difference! It gives the secret of *Indian Restaurant Cooking* – that particularly interesting and distinctive variety that is served in Indian restaurants all over the world.

Kris Dhillon writes with the authority of an accomplished Indian restaurateur, with many years of experience and thousands of satisfied customers. Most chefs guard closely the secret of their basic curry sauce, but here Kris Dhillon reveals all, and offers you the opportunity to reproduce that elusive taste, in your own kitchen.

AN INDIAN HOUSEWIFE'S RECIPE BOOK
Laxmi Khurana demolishes the myth that Indian cookery is cumbersome and time-consuming. She presents simple and economical family recipes made from ingredients and spices which are widely available.

Not only are curries featured, but there is an array of starters, snacks, raitas, chutneys, pickles and sweets. Everything, in fact, that characterises Indian cookery for people all over the world.

AUTHENTIC INDIAN COOKERY
Shelina Jetha's book contains family recipes which have been passed down the generations and between friends. From starters through main course dishes to sweets, with drinks, breads and accompaniments along the way, it will help you to create an authentic Indian meal in your own home.

CHINESE COOKERY SECRETS
How to Cook Chinese Restaurant Food at Home

Deh-Ta Hsiung shares his life-long knowledge of Chinese *restaurant* cooking to help you successfully reproduce your favourite meals at home – from a simple, single dish to an elaborate grand feast. He shows you each crucial stage of preparation to enable you to recreate the harmonious blending of subtle flavours, delicate textures, aromas, colours and shapes that are the hallmarks of authentic Chinese restaurant cooking.

SLOW COOKING PROPERLY EXPLAINED

The standard cookery book on slow cookers. Designed for those who are buying (or thinking of buying) their first slow cooker, as well as for the more experienced user. It contains over 100 recipes for tasty and nourishing dishes.

THE BIG OCCASION COOK BOOK

If you're organising a get-together for family and friends and don't know how to feed them all, then Jan Arkless can help you. She's compiled ten menus for those special occasions when you've got to feed a large number of guests. The recipes range from feeding 12 to 48 people, so whatever number you're entertaining there's something that will suit your needs.

HOW TO BOIL AN EGG

If you don't consider yourself a cook, this book is for you! It tells you how to boil an egg – and how to poach, scramble or fry it; it tells you how to prepare vegetables and about different meats and how to get all the elements of a meal ready to eat at the same time. It takes you from the very basics of cooking right through to the mysteries of "Sunday lunch". So, although most of the recipes are designed to feed one, there is scope for entertaining too, as you get more confident about your abilities in the kitchen.

NO MEAT FOR ME, PLEASE!

Jan Arkless's book contains a wealth of good advice and sumptuous recipes for the busy cook who has a vegetarian in the family. The recipe instructions are mostly given in quantities suitable for a single portion so that the book is also of value to the vegetarian who lives alone.

THE RIGHT WAY TO MAKE JAMS

This book tells you all you need to know to produce delicious home-made produce. It contains recipes for all the more usual fruit and vegetable jams, as well as some for out-of-the-ordinary ones, and includes recipes for conserves, marmalades, curds, pickles, chutneys and ketchups.

RIGHT WAY
PUBLISHING POLICY

HOW WE SELECT TITLES

RIGHT WAY consider carefully every deserving manuscript. Where an author is an authority on his subject but an inexperienced writer, we provide first-class editorial help. The standards we set make sure that every **RIGHT WAY** book is practical, easy to understand, concise, informative and delightful to read. Our specialist artists are skilled at creating simple illustrations which augment the text wherever necessary.

CONSISTENT QUALITY

At every reprint our books are updated where appropriate, giving our authors the opportunity to include new information.

FAST DELIVERY

We sell **RIGHT WAY** books to the best bookshops throughout the world. It may be that your bookseller has run out of stock of a particular title. If so, he can order more from us at any time – we have a fine reputation for "same day" despatch, and we supply any order, however small (even a single copy), to any bookseller who has an account with us. We prefer you to buy from your bookseller, as this reminds him of the strong underlying public demand for **RIGHT WAY** books. Readers who live in remote places, or who are housebound, or whose local bookseller is unco-operative, can order direct from us by post.

FREE

If you would like an up-to-date list of all **RIGHT WAY** titles currently available, send a stamped self-addressed envelope to
ELLIOT RIGHT WAY BOOKS,
LOWER KINGSWOOD, TADWORTH, SURREY,
KT20 6TD,U.K.
or visit our web site at www.right-way.co.uk